In Practice

Paul Hyett

With a forew

Cartoons by Louis Hellman

D0813647

In memoriam
Josephine Hyett
14th June 1930 – 8th September 1990

ISBN: 1 870308 33 6

Published by Emap Construct, 151 Rosebery Avenue, London EC1R 4GB.
Printed by BMK Printers, Dagenham, Essex. Copywright © Emap Construct 2000.
All rights reserved. No part of this publication may be reproduced in any format, or stored in any
retrieval system, or transmitted in any form or by any means, without the prior permission of the
publisher.

Contents

PART FOUR: UNDERSTANDING LEGISLATION

PART FIVE: HANDLING DISPUTES

PART SIX: SIMPLE MISTAKES TO AVOID

Foreword

Piers Gough

Paul Hyett's engagement with the world of architecture is mind-boggling. An RIBA Council member, education visiting board member, an Architectural Association committee member, an adjudicator and a professional witness, all alongside being a full time partner in practice. Plus, with his wife Sue he has a fully all-happening three-son family. On top of all this he finds time to write the most incredibly well informed, erudite and useful column across all these aspects of architecture every week in the Architects' Journal.

To be Treasurer of anything is usually a thankless and over-extended task. To be Treasurer of the Architectural Association is the kind of knife-edge job that I witnessed Paul executing with deft dedication, while managing to deflect praise onto everyone else involved. Passionate about education, he has made the world his portfolio while he reviewed those of schools in Latin America, the Far East and seemingly anywhere that enjoys RIBA validation. He is meanwhile arguing for greater emphasis on sustainability in education as well as for the much-cherished freedom to experiment and self-educate found at the AA.

In designing such buildings as the Fire Research Testing Station for the Building Research Establishment, he shows his fascination at the other end of the scale in the detailed way buildings are actually put together. Spells in the office of Cedric Price (at the same time as Will Alsop) and later as a partner of Nick Lacey have given him first-hand insight into the workings of avant garde thought and design, as well as the detailed delights of (in no particular order), copyright, arbitration, legal complexity, invention and responsibility. Every time I meet him he recommends some book he is reading, not, as one might expect on the new Part L, but on completely different subjects, be it dirigibles or the cosmos or philosophy.

This collection of essays is thus suffused with Paul's extraordinary knowledge, insight and continually enquiring mind. He is not afraid to take on the establishment, for example through his crusade against unregistered American architects, nor to scare the hell out of us with his dissection of our more onerous responsibilities. All this is done with a lovely dry humour which of course makes his pieces all the more readable and digestible. Should this make him seem like some impossible paragon of how an engaged professional should be? So be it. Should it make him seem impossibly aloof and superior? That would be quite wrong. Paul is also delightful, easy-going company who palpably enjoys the success of others.

Introduction

Paul Hyett

Architectural practice is a tough game, requiring wide knowledge, experience and skill. It's tough in medium- and larger-sized offices, where the demands of team management and information co-ordination intensify as the modern property world operates to ever faster programmes against seemingly ever tighter profit margins.

And it's tough in the smaller practices, particularly for sole practitioners who, single-handed, have to keep up with new procedures (such as CDM and Adjudication), new codes of practice, and new methods of procurement – all in the context of widespread competition and constantly reducing fee returns.

Against this background, skills and competence of builders and tradesmen decline, senior personnel in contracting companies seem more interested and knowledgeable about administration and constraints than materials and construction, and disputes and litigation are ever more prevalent.

Practice is therefore not only a tough game – it's a high-risk activity. But we can reduce the risks. An old boss of mine, the engineer Alan Baxter, once said: 'The same problems keep coming but the trouble is, they come in different disguises.'

With that in mind, I have prepared this book to help practitioners. It is largely based on my own 25 years of working experience, which began in my father's office, a small practice of two sole principals: James Herriotts of the architectural world, with work throughout Herefordshire and the Welsh border country. Since then my career has included time as a sole practitioner in my own right, before beginning the long process of developing an office with my partners. Now, following restructuring into a company and a subsequent merger, I find myself the chairman of a firm of some 60 people, with offices in London and Newcastle. But the lessons that I learned early in my career largely apply to our work today (though of course we go on learning all the time). The basic objectives remain the same: establish the brief; prepare accurate and reliable information; plan the critical path through the job; resource appropriately; and deliver a project that is technically sound, to programme and within cost targets. And, of course, make it architecture.

I have also been informed by my experience as an expert witness, regularly investigating and reporting on claims against architects. Most of these relate to alleged administrative failures or technical problems, ranging in size from very small disputes to claims of many millions of pounds. I can't always get architects 'off the hook' – and anyway that is not the job of an expert – but I do try to explain to the Court what has actually gone wrong, the real cost of putting it right, and how the blame should properly be apportioned. Architects are not usually as culpable as the plaintiff's lawyers would suggest.

This book has been divided into six sections, starting with good practice and risk management. I then move on to fee appointments and getting paid, managing the office, and understanding legislation. There is then a section on handling disputes, and a final section on simple mistakes to avoid. All the pieces published here were originally prepared during my five years stint as a weekly columnist for the Architects' Journal – a job I loved.

This is not a complete practice manual, and it certainly won't make you a better designer. But it will help you to spot, and with luck avoid, many common problems. If you learn from my experiences you may be able to maintain a constant course through the waters of professional practice. But keep a good look-out: there are always sharp rocks lurking just beneath the surface. And let me know of any new threats that come to light: you can contact me via e-mail: hsw@dial.pipex.com, or write to me at 36-37 Featherstone Street, London EC1Y 8QZ.

Staying out of trouble is important: it allows you to focus on what you like doing most – making good architecture. I hope this book will both help and amuse you.

Acknowledgements

Paul Finch and Ruth Slavid took me to lunch one day and offered me the job of regular columnist at The Architects' Journal. As a result of their confidence, and patience, I learned any skills that I have as a writer.

Isabel Allen, my current editor, and all my colleagues at The Architects' Journal, have ensured that my involvement with journalism has been both a challenge and a pleasure.

Adam Whiteley and Ian Salisbury, as partners in practice, have contributed immeasurably to any success that my column has enjoyed.

Cedric Price has been, as always, a friend and a constant inspiration. Shobie Patel, my secretary, has been patience personified.

Then there is the debt I owe to those that I have worked with, especially Marco Goldschmied, and all those practitioners who have provided the rich range of experiences that I have drawn upon as material for my writing. And of course the readers who, through their comments and letters, have made my task so rewarding.

And finally, my old mate John Lyall must not be forgotten: he prompted me to write this book.

Dear friends, I thank you all!

PART 1

Professionalism, good practice, and risk management

What makes a professional

'Professional' is today an increasingly misunderstood and abused word. As architects, subject to high levels of responsibility and client expectation, we should give careful consideration to the conditions necessary for delivering a professional service. They are becoming ever more elusive.

We read of professional footballers, athletes, rally drivers and even professional car salesman. In the first three examples professional merely indicates paid activity – in the last the term is meaningless. The salesman's objective is to maximise profits. Some are, of course, more reputable than others, but their first duty is to their company, not the purchaser.

Brokers, by comparison, are intermediaries, whilst craftsmen undertake skilled tasks for their employers. But the essence of a professional service is the application of knowledge, skill and judgement that is primarily in a client's best interest. Sometimes the work may even be beyond the client's comprehension.

Medicine, possibly the second oldest profession, offers many clear examples of professionalism. The surgeon must advise his patient where a hip replacement is unwarranted, perhaps recommending physiotherapy instead, thus foregoing all opportunity of financial gain. The patient's interests accordingly take precedence over any commercial gain for the surgeon. Traders, on the other hand, may offer discounts for complete hip and pelvis replacements in the interests of sales.

Some readers will think these comments out-dated, even outrageous. But such distinctions are very important, particularly at a time when our capacity to deliver the quality of professional service that the courts expect of us (if we are unfortunate enough to be sued) is increasingly threatened by those who meddle with our terms of engagement.

Back to the medical analogy: nobody expects surgeons to perform open heart surgery without anaesthetic, a sterile environment, appropriate resources and support, proper preparation and adequate time. By contrast, the architect's working arrangements are frequently adjusted, abbreviated, interrupted, shortened, or restructured (often without consultation by QS firms or project managers), in ways that seriously damage our capacity to exercise professional competence. Do not let this happen to you – such excuses provide no defence in court!

Only recently I learned of an architect who had been commissioned by the developer for scheme design, novated to the builder for production information, and then novated back to the developer again for settlement of the final account! You can guess what that game was all about. Another architect saw no conflict in acting for both developer and builder simultaneously. Try telling that to the judge!

Make no mistake: as architect it is your responsibility to establish and maintain conditions conducive to delivering a competent professional service; you must not let others make arrangements that adversely affect your capacity to achieve the standards expected of a reasonably competent architect. Either negotiate appropriate terms – fees, programme, responsibilities – or, difficult as it may be, you should resign. Otherwise, the costs to you, your PI insurer, and our profession, may ultimately be too heavy to bear.

Architectural education continues to shift towards design at the cost of technical and practice-related areas. The Courts offer no concessions for these trends. So, where necessary, get wise! Make sure you establish and maintain the knowledge, skills and conditions appropriate to the delivery of a professional service. Don't commit a professional foul.

Sharp practice or malpractice?

Many years ago, I designed a scheme that included a loft conversion which the client intended to use as a child's bedroom. Unfortunately, the 1972 Building Regulations required minimum ceiling heights to be provided over a prescribed proportion of a habitable room's floor area. Having consulted the wonderful illustrated Guide to the Building Regulations, by A J Elder, I was in no doubt: the application would be refused. I pointed out to the client that the standards could not be met without restructuring the roof. However, if the space was marked as a 'boxroom', not a 'bedroom', consent would be forthcoming. Weighing up the alternatives, in terms of cost and compromise, the client decided to proceed with a conversion to provide a boxroom, which I suspect he ultimately used as a bedroom.

Did I do wrong? The ARB might like to think so, but I would say that I explained in writing the limitations on use. If the client thereafter chose to breach those limitations, that was his prerogative and a matter between him and the enforcement officer. Either way, I lost no sleep over the matter, for the space provisions would be better than within many delightful cottage bedrooms in the area.

The issue is, of course, now academic. Under subsequent sweeping reforms to construction legislation, such restrictions on space standards were 'lifted', so what does it matter anyway? Well, it matters a lot because as professionals we have a duty to comply with the legislation of the day. Insofar as this arrangement didn't comply, I could be criticised. But I was instructed to design a boxroom . . .

Youthful enthusiasm had of course spurred me on, but caution in these circumstances is essential. Over-zealous endeavours on behalf of a client can lead to tears, not to mention very serious litigation.

In a recent case, a surveyor (not an architect) had arranged for major demolition and alteration work to be carried out to a listed building without having obtained consent under the Planning (Listed Building and Conservation Areas) Act 1990. He advised the client, in writing, that the work should be carried on 'behind closed doors' using a 'softly, softly, incremental approach'. Injunctions duly followed.

Incompetence? Negligence? No, this was simply gross misconduct. The surveyor and builder had each knowingly committed a criminal act. Sadly, and despite his ignorance, the unfortunate client was also implicated.

In another case, an architect submitted an application under Building Regulations which included an 'as existing' drawing showing a staircase to an attic where no stairs existed. He explained in a subsequent court case that there was insufficient room in this old house for a complying staircase, so deception had been his tactic for securing consent. Again, this is just the sort of gross misconduct that the ARB's disciplinary committee should be dealing with. No proper attention had been given to means of escape, doors to lower floors had not been upgraded to the required fire rating, and the architect had wilfully misled the building inspector.

The line between sharp practice and malpractice can be very fine but it does exist. When events fall against you, that line may be judged by others very harshly indeed – especially if a coroner is involved.

Specification: the essential art form

Arriving late – no fault of Virgin Trains – to join an AJ panel during the Interbuild Exhibition, I was confronted, still out of breath, with a request to round up an Internet discussion: should advertisers use Internet? Do architects research products there?

Despite a sceptical audience, I remain convinced that in its mature state Internet will provide specifiers with an unparalleled service for rapid sourcing and retrieval of manufacturers' and suppliers' data. With ever-shorter contract lead-in times, and the inevitable ongoing development of building products, it surely makes sense to access accurate and up-to-date product information through the net. Suppliers simply must keep pace with ever more sophisticated demands for an on-line facility enabling product comparisons and immediate data retrieval. But the net is only as good as its users – who must establish web-sites with enthusiasm and imagination: it isn't good enough routinely to utilise tired old brochure material.

Other questions during the session related to the specifier's authority – ie how to ensure that manufacturers secure orders where specifications clearly stipulate their products. (This process is increasingly at risk through the growing tendency amongst consultants to avoid nomination of components, suppliers and sub-contractors.) Coming from a school which believes absolutely in the role of architect as specifier, I see the abrogation of this responsibility as dangerous for both client and architect for two reasons.

First, specification is an essential part of design and is an art form in its own right. The character of space is heavily dependent on the products and materials that form it – designers should therefore maintain a controlling input from spatial organisation through to construction and component specification. Architects simply cannot allow the builder or QS unilaterally to assume this role if they wish to maintain a hold on design consistency through the production stage. Design quality is immediately traded where this involvement is lost, even on the best of projects. Schools of architecture should take note!

The second reason concerns litigation: the poor architect is time and again dragged into disputes when product defects lead to building failures and claims. Even where only a general performance specification is given, attempts may be made to sue the architect by suggesting that he has subsequently 'approved' the detailed specifications put forward by the contractor or specialist sub-contractor. Furthermore, by certifying payments, practical completion and, most onerous of all, final certification, the architect may expose himself to criticisms and claims, however unjustly, whenever faults arise.

Certainly for traditional methods of building and contracts it is in the interest of both client and PI insurer that architects remain centre stage with respect to specification work. Clients expect buildings to be 'right first time' and 'fit for purpose'. This is best achieved through a robust partnership between product and material manufacturers on the one hand and architects (who have the knowledge and skill required for the processes of research, and material/component assessment) on the other. Indeed, the contribution of manufacturers and suppliers is invaluable as it complements and updates the general specification knowledge base upon which the architect, and of course the construction industry at large, both heavily depend.

Sadly, little respect now exists for the 'art' of specification writing – indeed nowhere in an architect's formal education is there any attention given to this important area of the profession's work. Architecture itself is the poorer for this state of affairs, architects more vulnerable, and clients less well served.

Keeping tabs on your sub-consultants

The increasing preference of clients to appoint a single consultant, who in turn must sub-contract work outside his discipline to other consultants, produces real difficulties often overlooked in the haste to secure new work.

Under these arrangements clients are, of course, able to agree a single fee arrangement for all consultancy work involved in a project, payable to one firm only. That 'lead' firm must negotiate competitive terms with other consultants, define their briefs, ultimately pay those other consultants, and deal with (and assume the risk for) any claims that arise for additional fees. While clearly convenient for clients, such arrangements can be a nightmare for consultants – whether appointed as 'employers' or merely as 'sub-consultants'.

In one such situation, where an architect was a sub-consultant, the client refused to pay additional fees which arose from changed instructions. The engineering firm which had sub-contracted the architectural services would not press the matter on behalf of the architect for fear of threatening its own interest in subsequent commissions with the same client. As the architect had no direct appointment with the client his sole recourse was to sue the engineer – his fellow consultant.

Another case involved an architect sub-contracted by a QS for housing association work. He resigned because the QS introduced procedures and sequences of work that put the architect at risk under the terms of his collateral warranty to the client. Indeed, other professionals in this position (particularly QS firms), have been adept at setting up 'home-spun' warranties in which, effectively, they attempt to side-step responsibility for sub-consultant's work.

While there exist various standard forms of collateral warranty that can be given by consultants, these have been drafted in favour of funding institutions, purchasers and tenants. There is not yet a model warranty for sub-consultants' work in favour of the client. However, good news: the RIBA is reviewing this area as I write.

In the meantime, here is some useful advice if you sub-contract work to other consultants:

● Don't permit sub-consultancy terms that vary from those which you agree with the client. In particular do not allow sub-consultants to reduce their liability, or make fee claims for additional services, that you in turn cannot recover.

● Don't let sub-consultants take instructions from other parties.

● Ensure adequate PI cover is available from the sub-consultants and that your own policy covers your extended liabilities.

● Make it a condition of appointment that the sub-consultant enters into a collateral warranty arrangement with the client.

● The terms of that warranty should be explicit and should refer to the sub-agreement between the consultants which should be attached.

If you are a sub-consultant:

● Ensure that your appointment terms do not impose unsatisfactory arrangements on you about intervals of payment or unreasonable conditions for payment (such as 'pay when paid'). This is very important: non-payment by the client may render your account with the employing consultant void.

● Make sure the consultant that employs you instructs any variations to the scope of your work in writing, and that appropriate fees are agreed before such work is started.

While they are increasing in popularity, and many of us accept them, these methods of appointment are potentially dangerous, so beware.

Sub-contractor design liabilities

Next time that you are involved in a project where a specialist sub-contractor has a design responsibility, think carefully about your own position in the event of their failure – you may have more liabilities than you expect, and more than are suggested under the RIBA's Standard Form of Agreement (SFA/92).

Clause 4.2.5 states: 'The Client shall hold any Specialist and not the Architect responsible for the products and materials supplied by the Specialist and for the competence, proper execution, and performance of the work with which such Specialists are entrusted.' Perfectly clear you may think. But if so, why in case after case where specialist sub-contractor firms are deemed to have failed in their design responsibility is the poor old architect dragged into expensive litigation?

It's all too easy for the plaintiff to cite the architect as a second defendant in an action which is brought primarily against the specialist sub-contractor – a 'catch-all' tactic which provides additional security through the architect's PI in the event that the sub-contractor goes belly-up.

That said, when formulating a claim it is often difficult to differentiate responsibility between the various parties in matters of design co-ordination: careful investigation may well be necessary where problems of co-ordination exist – between say curtain wall and steel frame – in order to establish liability for error.

But what of the apparently open-and-shut cases where there is an inherent design fault with the product supplied by the specialist. For example, the panel cladding system that 'bows' and looks unsightly; the curtain walling installation that leaks; or the wardrobe system that disintegrates following its installation into that top-grade hotel project.

I had such a case myself when a curtain wall system began to leak badly, shortly after handover of the building. The full wrath of J R Knowles (who frequently act as claims consultants) was unleashed upon us, and much time was expended in defending ourselves.

Our argument was simple: the curtain wall system was a specialist item. We had set out clear performance criteria in terms of issues such as protection against solar gain and thermal performance, and we had given accurate dimensional information. We had received and commented on the specialist's drawings and specification with respect to these issues, but we had not assumed responsibility for the gasket arrangements which provided the seal at mullion/transom junctions where the problems had arisen. Our arguments were accepted and the case against us was dropped.

However, in a similar dispute involving a newly qualified architect I was recently advised that the test a court would apply was whether the issue of alleged failure related to an area of expertise that an architect of reasonable competence would be expected to hold.

Take lifts. If the lift car failed to function as a result of an engineering problem within the motor, that would be outside the normal experience of an architect. But if the carpet peeled off the walls because inappropriate adhesive was used, or the walnut veneer deteriorated because it was insufficiently durable for the purpose, the architect might be dragged into the dispute because these matters are supposed to fall within his routine expertise.

Of course, it's not all over at that stage, and a successful defence may be made, but the cost of defence and heartache involved can be considerable, to say nothing of ongoing PI premium increases which can be incurred while liability is being determined.

So, next time you seek to rely on SFA clause 4.2.5 think carefully: much is at stake. Don't let the client, QS, or project manager land you with some cheapskate and incompetent firm who might suck you into a mire of controversy. And, even if a good firm is appointed, make sure that you scrutinise those parts of their work which lie within your experience carefully, and ensure that a client/sub-contractor form of warranty is in place.

Finally, of course, comment critically as appropriate, but don't ever 'approve' any sub-contractor drawings or design proposals.

Controlling cost and programme

Nicola Horlick, the clever and energetic financial consultant who combines a dazzling City career with the role of successful wife and mum, is now to be seen on the new PEPs adverts which litter London's stations. A carefully crafted piece of marketing, the advert shows three sober faces: the confident Nicola; the young and highly groomed John Richards; and in case John's too clever, Peter Seabrook, his cautious smile underpinning a furrowed brow and receding hairline. Personal investment is obviously so complex that you need a creative high-flyer (John), a tough and determined operator (Nicola), and an experienced old bird (Peter), in order to sort this territory out.

Houses, like PEPs, also represent big investment. Indeed an extension of £45,000, is more than most people put into an investment plan in a lifetime. So, what kind of message is put out by the 65% of architects who, as small practitioners, operate extensively in this field of work? How well trained, and how knowledgeable are they on issues of finance? What help can they give their clients in preparing or presenting the case for a loan? Can they arrange finance? What contacts do they have?

Think of all those other purchases: television, fridge, washing machine or new car; the factory supplied conservatory; the new fitted kitchen, bedroom or study . . . Purchases as small as a few hundred pounds, through to £20,000 plus, all come with advice upon and easy access to finance. No hassle . . . sign here say the eager salesman. It's all part of the service.

And architects? Most of us expect even our domestic clients to find all the construction capital as well as the £3,000 odd for our services without any support whatsoever, when most of them need loan facilities even to convert the attic.

Now think of our training. How much financial knowledge does your average architect have at graduation? What does he/she understand of the language that lenders will speak? Can he impart confidence to the client's bank or building society that he will control construction costs, comply with budgets and ensure investment returns.

At graduation they will know nothing of books like Ivor Seeley's

'Building Economics' (now in its fourth edition), its glossy cover showing Hopkins' Inland Revenue Centre under construction. Sixteen chapters deal, in logical ordered fashion, with such essential territories as 'Cost implications of design variables/Effect of site conditions on building costs/Approximate estimating techniques/Cost control procedures at design stage . . . and at construction stage/Valuation processes/Life cycle costing' and so on. This, together with techniques of management, is of course the staple diet of the QS in training.

The point here is that the ability to predetermine project costs and ensure satisfactory financial control is essential to any investment decision. That involves, whether at small domestic scale, or on large commercial projects, a level of skill and experience that is simply not taught, acquired, or discussed in our schools of architecture. It also involves a concern and responsibility that is usually discouraged and frequently dismissed in the most cavalier of fashions during studio crits and seminars.

Of course, most who visit the current AJ small project exhibition at the RIBA and enjoy the talent, while marvelling at the richness of ingenuity in the work, would think all is well, especially in the small works arena. But, and without intending any slur on such wonderful exhibits, how many times do we hear of projects small and large that dazzling architectural outcomes have been heavily marred by unhappy financial outcomes?

Buildings represent enormous investment, and those who wish to enjoy responsibility for their delivery must complement their design contribution with appropriate supporting inputs, including monetary skills. And just think what potential exists for far greater penetration of the important market in small projects for any architects who can offer reliable fiscal advice, as well as reasonable surety of financial outcome, with access to project finance.

Site inspections – for what?

Alleged failure to properly 'supervise' construction work is still a common claim against architects. 'Ah,' I hear many of you say, 'we are not responsible for supervision – merely for periodic inspection.'

Reference to supervision is, of course, a hangover from pre-1971 appointment terms. Thereafter, the little A5 purple 'Conditions of Engagement' stipulated that the architect 'shall make such periodic visits to the site as he considers necessary to inspect generally the progress and quality of the work . . .' Note that this reduced responsibility nevertheless implied an obligation to assess the necessity and frequency of visits.

Thereafter, the 'Architect's appointment' (1982) stipulated under clause 3.10 that visits should be made 'at intervals appropriate to the stage of construction . . .' – a quite different requirement.

Under clause 3.1.1 of SFA/92 the obligation was again varied, this time to read 'make such visits to the works as the Architect at the date of the Appointment reasonably expected to be necessary'. This not only conflicts with earlier appointment terms, and, arguably, with the industry's expectations based on precedent, it also conflicted with Schedule Two, paragraph K-L/08 within the same document, which repeated the duty to visit the site 'At intervals appropriate to the stage of construction . . .'

Lawyers have earned a fortune while the true extent of these duties has been disputed in the Courts. And every time case law comes near to establishing an interpretation, our noble profession rewrites its appointment documents. Predictably, we've done it again with the publication of SFA/99.

And, true to form, we've delivered the lawyers another gravy train, and ourselves a real nightmare! Clause 2.8 of SFA/99 retains the SFA/92 obligation to make such visits as 'the Architect at the date of the appointment reasonably expected to be necessary'. But paragraph 1 of Work Stage K of the Services Supplement states 'Make Visits (sic) to the works in connection with the Architect's design'.

What does that mean? How often? At what stages? With what purpose? With what level of detail? And note that the phrase 'to inspect generally the progress and quality of the work', with its limiting qualification, has vanished.

So architects, now denied the protection of the precious words 'inspect generally,' will suffer as lawyers acting for clients inevitably argue that our responsibilities have been substantially extended. Defence lawyers will, of course, run the weaker case that the purpose of the visits is non-specific (general interest, pleasure, photography, even curiosity or a picnic!) But such arguments are pretty hopeless.

In another incredible blunder that further confuses the situation, the SFA/99 Services Supplement (side B!) describes the tender and construction activities as 'Work Stages A-G'. (Think about it!) And on page 9, Stage E is retitled 'Final Proposals'. ('E' was previously 'Detail Design' under SFA/92). If you find all that confusing, ask yourself what 'Detailed Droposals' (sic) might mean (SFA/99 page 9).

The seriousness of all this should not be underestimated. Varying the descriptions of the architect's duties has significant legal implications, and should not be done whimsically. If such changes are, however, either unavoidable or essential, replacement documents must be consistent and clear throughout – as opposed to inconsistent, ambiguous, and compromised by typographical errors, as has too often been the case.

Furthermore, architects must adjust their service in order to comply with their new obligations – difficult when, as with site inspection, those obligations are unclear.

In her book 'The Legal Obligations of the Architect' Andrea Burns (assisted by AJ columnist Kim Franklyn) wrote: 'In actions against architects, plaintiffs rely heavily on the duty of inspection to prosecute cases of poor construction.' That was in 1994, and Burns went on to suggest that as long as appointment terms include the words 'intervals appropriate to the stage of construction' that reliance would continue, for who could define what would constitute appropriate intervals?

Well, lawyers can stop worrying about all that now, as SFA/99 gives them the welcome opportunity to ponder instead just what making visits 'in connection with the Architect's design' might mean. Sadly for us, many lawyers will retire very fat on the fees they make arguing that one out.

You and the clerk of works

I recently suggested that the growing tendency under modern procurement methods (D&B etc.) to exclude architects from site inspection is leaving clients very exposed. Last week I considered the architect's inspection duties under traditional forms of appointment, and noted that SFA/99 generates unwelcome ambiguity in this matter. Here, I will look at the role of Site Inspectors; a task traditionally fulfilled by that frequently hated, maligned, and bullied figure, the clerk of works.

This interest stems from a recent litigation in which an architect's defence alleged that multiple serious faults discovered, post-construction, in a hospital project should have been spotted by the CoW, who had been in attendance full time throughout the construction phase.

This argument seemed all the more robust because the CoW was permanently employed by the hospital's own estates department. Why, claimed the defence, should the architect be held responsible for detailed inspection work which had gone way beyond his duties under item 08 of Work Stages K-L, under which he was only required to visit at appropriate intervals 'to determine that (the works were) being executed generally in accordance with the contract documents?'

Sadly, the architect's position was weakened both through case law (which has largely established that an architect is responsible for the inadequacies and failures of the CoW) and though clause 3.3.3 of SFA/92, which states: 'All Site Staff shall be under the direction and control of the Architect'. (It was, I presume, intended that the term 'Site Staff' referred to site architects and CoWs as opposed to site engineers and the builders' employees – but again, the poor drafting of SFA documents can be seen to have left architects deeply at risk. Those who serve us in this respect really do need to wake up and sharpen up.)

SFA/99 remains vague on this matter. Clause 3.10 states that (where appointed) 'Site Inspectors shall be under the direction of the Lead Consultant' despite it being the duty of the client to 'appoint and pay them under separate agreements'. However, and in apparent conflict with 3.10, Clause 3.11 goes on to state that 'in respect of any work or services in connection with the Project' the client shall 'hold such person (and, by implication, not the architect) responsible for the competence and performance of his services'. This might wash for other consultants such as the structural engineer, but it apparently doesn't work with respect to CoW.

Useful guidance on this matter can be found in 'Design Liability in the Construction Industry' in which D L Cornes considers whether delegation to CoWs and other inspectors of the 'duty to supervise (sic) relieves (the architect) of part or the whole of his duties to supervise such that he incurs no liability if there is a breach of duty by the person to whom the supervision has been delegated'.

Concluding that an overriding principle applies that the architect 'will not necessarily be held liable for failing to . . . detect every minor piece of poor workmanship', Cornes advises that: 'the architect cannot delegate matters of importance so as to divest himself of responsibility, but he can delegate matters of minor importance'.

A useful test is offered on the basis of case law which suggests that the architect will usually be liable for breach of duty with respect to his site inspection role if:

● He purports to delegate a matter which he should not have delegated, but rather, should have seen to himself.

● He purports to delegate where he should have given instructions as to how the supervision was to be carried out, and he failed to give such instructions.

● He relies on an unreliable clerk of works or resident engineer when he knows (them) to be unreliable.

Professional practice is a tough game! Don't accept these responsibilities without being paid properly during the construction phase. If the scope of your service is limited, you should explicitly shed your responsibilities accordingly – don't get sued for work you aren't even being paid for!

The limits of professional liability

Clauses, 6.1, 6.2 and 6.3, within the SFA/92 Memorandum of Agreement attempt to provide for the limiting of an architect's liability in the event of a claim being made against him.

SFA/99, presented to RIBA Council at the January meeting, replaces these clauses with a very simple new line that reads: 'Limit of liability: £x'

Will this wash with the courts? They have traditionally taken scant account of such limitations where the client is a private individual without expertise in development work, or in the appointment of construction consultants. So on past record probably not with 'private' clients.

However, a recent ruling by the Hon Mr Justice Dyson has important implications in this respect. The case under consideration related to a client who claimed damages against an architect for alleged negligence and/or breach of contract in connection with the design and construction of a new house.

There was, within the Memorandum of Agreement under SFA/92, a stipulated limit of £250,000 liability and the judge gave a decision on two issues: did clauses 6.1 to 6.3 apply to all the pleaded cases of the action? And did clauses 6.1 to 6.3 satisfy the test of reasonableness under UCTA (Unfair Contract Terms Act)?

The judge ruled that in this case 'Clause 6 and in particular the limitation (of £250,000) in clause 6.2, satisfied the test of reasonableness, and applies to all the Plaintiff's causes of action.'

In coming to his decision as to the test of 'reasonableness' Dyson stated that it was common ground that the Plaintiff dealt with the Defendant as a consumer within the meaning of section 12 of UCTA. He quoted from those provisions as follows: '. . . regard shall be had to . . . (a) the resources which the architect could expect to be available to him for the purpose of meeting the liability should it arise; and (b) how far it was open to the architect to cover himself by insurance.'

Referring to *Flamar Interocean* v *Denmore* (1990), the judge stated that the guidelines which were of particular relevance in his deliberations were: 'the strength of the bargaining positions of the parties relative to each other . . . whether the customer received an inducement to agree the term . . . and whether the customer knew or ought reasonably to have known of the existence and extent of the term.'

Stating that the burden was on the defendant to satisfy the requirement of reasonableness; and reaching the conclusion that the defendant had discharged that burden, the judge observed that the £250,000 limit was not an arbitrary figure, but was the architect's assessment of the likely cost of construction: furthermore, because the plaintiff could have instructed any architect, he was in a stronger bargaining position than the defendant. Finally, noted the judge, both the plaintiff and his solicitor had been aware prior to entering the agreement that clause 6 existed.

Squire & Co, solicitors specialising in PI litigation who acted for the architects in this case, suggest that architects take care when imposing any clause that restricts liability. However, it must, as in the case reported above, meet the test of 'reasonableness' if it is to receive the support of the courts.

Architects' Journal 11.2.99

Unusual risks and PI cover

Initially worried, I had learned to live with the 'bulge' to the flank wall of our Hackney home: it expanded and contracted with the afternoon sun, causing a crack to open and close in an alarming way.

Locals, who still sang war-time songs to the pub-piano next door, remembered the bomb blast which had destroyed a nearby house and caused our bulge. They had seen roofs lift and walls 'oscillate' – there was even a surreal photograph of bedroom curtains swept out over a wall plate and subsequently pinned when a roof resettled!.

The blocking piece supporting our hallway beam had twisted onto the diagonal during 'negative' pressure. That's how we found it some 40 years later during our 'DIY' renovations. Engineer Alan Conisbee specified structural repairs and marvelled that the Victorian fabric could accommodate such blast damage.

The recent Docklands explosion is a different affair: our client's 'high-tech' steel framed office suffered extensive damage when the bomb exploded 300 metres away. The results were quite unexpected – unless you are an expert in the dynamics of explosions. Issues arising for architects include professional indemnity insurance, staff safety during inspections, strategies for repair, and professional risk management.

Insurance is a mine-field. Our standard PI policy covers bomb damage repairs, which our broker quipped is now a 'normal service'. (With £1.1 billion of London damage occurring in only four years he has a point.). More complex is staff protection: our Employer's Liability policy only covers us where our negligence is proved – otherwise such claims fall to the building owner's third party liability insurance. Would injury consequent on delayed events – perhaps a ceiling collapse – involve our negligence for sending staff into danger? If so can special cover be obtained? Such claims against owners may fail where policies exclude terrorism, now common since the Bishopsgate bomb. So: undertake a thorough insurance review before starting this type of work.

Safety is crucial: set up restricted zones for client staff and the public; arrange temporary support and where necessary partial or total demolition. Consider working methods: Condam regulations may apply. Ensure the contractor carries adequate insurance: who pays if he sets the building on fire – what was it worth anyway? Such claims are a lawyer's paradise, but don't make it too easy for them.

Conduct a full survey before permanent repairs are organised: shock waves can even damage A/C equipment through ductwork. Identifying hidden damage involves understanding the structure's behaviour and response to the blast. If you need to open-up the fabric, remember your staff cover almost certainly excludes manual work away from the office: the builder must do it for you.

We found some permanent bending to pipework, while the blockwork formed brittle panels which had fractured and distorted. Northlights had occasionally shattered, otherwise all other glazing remained intact. There were water leaks but gas supplies remained secure.

Professional responsibilities need careful review: confirm your brief in writing. The client may not want a complete survey and may prefer to compromise over repairs. Subject to the building inspector's approval that is his prerogative, but the architect should limit his own risk by cautioning the client: unexpected problems may occur later.

No chances should, however, be taken over safety – it is better to resign than to compromise in this matter. Consideration should be given to modifying the building to mitigate the effect of any future bomb blasts, this may ease the client's insurance premiums but construction costs increase.

Establish the separate briefs and responsibilities of other consultants clearly – particularly the structural engineer and QS. Ask the engineer to affirm an adequate brief for his own work. Watch the QS: he'll be more confused than usual and contracts, cost planning and cost control in these situations need very careful attention.

As with bombs, bomb repair work is potentially very dangerous so be vigilant. Dig out your old AJ from 30.6.93 for your survival bag – it contains an excellent article on this type of work.

Watch out for skeletons

When asked if he had any skeletons in his cupboard, Alan Clark MP said: 'Dear boy, I can hardly close the door.' Jobs sometimes create skeletons for architects, as this story will reveal . . .

Some years ago, a loyal client returned to us with a commission for a new building when his screen-printing business outgrew the facilities that we had designed for him only a few years before. We were of course pleased and set to work, hoping to better reconcile the second time around the conflicting demands on space arising from the company's continued increases of market share, the anticipated growth of their business sector, and the economies arising through 'shrinking' technologies in screenprinting.

Two years later, the relocation complete, I learned that their old building (originally designed by us in the mid-80s) had been sold. Sadly, the purchaser was hit by the recession and went into receivership and I heard from friends living near the site that the building on which we had worked with such commitment and care was unoccupied, and being vandalised.

Then, some months later and out of the blue I received a telephone call from a company director who told me that his firm had just bought the building which was to be converted and expanded as their Birmingham headquarters – would we do the job? This was great news and to our further delight appointment terms were agreed that day – no fee haggling, they wanted us, simple as that!

And so, to the skeleton in my cupboard.

I knew that there had been occasional problems, over many years, during certain weather conditions. It seemed likely that there was an installation failure somewhere within the vapour barrier and that condensation was forming under the metal roof sheet and finding its way into the main entrance hall where it revealed itself through a steady drip. However, symptoms had been very intermittent and seemed to occur only when heavy overnight freezing was followed by bright sunshine on the south-facing roof slopes. Some years the drip returned, other years no problems were evident. Should I tell our new client?

This led us to review carefully the issues of responsibility for any defects in our earlier work. We knew of no problems other than this matter of condensation, but our contract and responsibilities for the original building were with our first client. Should I now seek to limit our liability to the alteration work to be commissioned by the building's new owner – ie expressly excluding our earlier design work? (Hardly the way to impress a new client, or to demonstrate confidence in our past services.) And what of the work of the other consultants? Alternatively, should we suggest that our new client commission us to carry out a conditions survey of the building and review of the previous architect's (our) work? Certainly this is something one would normally consider with any other alteration job.

We ultimately chose a middle course. Nothing was said about the intermittent fault with the vapour barrier. (I decided that as no problems had been reported for some four years that it was probably something that only occurred in freak weather conditions.)

On the big issue of limiting our liability to the new work only, we did nothing. Some would argue that architects should be firmer on matters like this and seek every opportunity to limit risk. Perhaps that is right, but it didn't make commercial sense to me to risk losing the client's confidence, and possibly the job, by trying expressly to exclude responsibility for work that to our knowledge had no problems. Either way, the new commission was finished without incident and the building has now been occupied for some five years without any reported defects in either the original fabric or the alteration work.

That said, be careful when revisiting past work – you inevitably open up a hornet's nest of liability issues.

Be precise and be polite

David Suitor's plea (AJ letters 14.10.99) that bad language should be kept out of 'any professional journal' must be right, but editors often face difficult choices in these matters.

For example, reporting in the legal case of Snook v Mannion, Judge Ormrod of the Queen's Bench Division had to review at appeal the meaning of the term 'fuck off'. The court's decision is important for everybody, especially those who wish to be clearly understood when making requests or giving instructions, so architects read on.

Mr Snook, having arrived home and parked his car in his drive, was confronted by two police officers who, having noticed his erratic driving, had pursued him in their squad car. Refusing a breathalyser test with the words 'fuck off', Snook was duly arrested and, following blood tests, was convicted by the local magistrates for drunken driving. His appeal defence, accepting his drunken state, was based solely on the principle that despite the defendant's 'request' that the police leave his premises, they had failed to do so. It was alleged that after the request had been made their 'presence on his driveway was illegal and any subsequent action (eg his arrest) would also be illegal'.

Apparently, unless we provide a locked gate to our drive, or maintain a clear sign such as 'Police Keep Out' prominently displayed, police officers, like the postman and anyone else, have an implied right to enter private property and continue to the front or back door in order to pursue their legitimate business. However, if asked to leave a driveway they must do so, as their uninvited presence on private property, even for purposes of arrest, requires a warrant, unless they have 'permission' to be there.

So the crucial issue in this case, which of course had to be reported in the legal journals in precise detail, was whether Snook had made his request clear. Was he terminating the police officers' implied licence to be on his property for their legal business, or was the term merely a vulgar expression which had contained no meaningful request or instructions?

Sensibly, counsel for the defendant did not seek to prove that the statement 'fuck off' was to be exclusively relied upon as an indication of

Snook's request. In a previous case this term had been viewed as an obscenity rather than a request (*Gilham* v *Breidenbach*).

Counsel said that Snook had made his intentions clear through his actions, as well as his words. In essence, it was claimed that the police officers must have realised that anyone rushing to the sanctuary of their drive would not wish to be breathalysed. The police officers accepted that Snook had told them to 'fuck off', but claimed that 'they had not gained any impression that the defendant was intimating to them that their licence to come onto his property was being revoked or that they were being asked to leave'.

In dismissing the appeal, Justice Ormrod said, 'ingenious as Mr Green's submission is, we must, with regret, reject it.' He concluded that the police had decided that Snook had not made his request clear – perhaps he was merely refusing to be breathalysed which, as an isolated act, he was not entitled to do.

The lesson of this story? Clearly not only is swearing offensive, as Mr Suitor's letter so properly points out, but it is also prone to misinterpretation. Whenever you make requests or give instructions, especially in your formal role as an architect, you should always be very precise. If Snook had said 'I withdraw the implied licence that you enjoy to enter my driveway – I require you to leave', the police would have been obliged to rush off for a warrant, allowing their 'quarry' to enjoy a further whisky or two before their return thus rendering their breathalyser test useless.

So, it appears that Mr Suitor gives us all good advice in his letter: bad language really doesn't pay. But it is sometimes necessary for an editor to print it in all its blue glory if an issue is to be properly reported . . .

Architects' Journal 18.11.99

PART 2

Appointments and getting the cash in

Pre-appointment foreplay

My parents were reasonably relaxed about my wife and me living together before marriage, but Mum did not want Auntie Gladys to know although my Nan was in on the whole affair from the beginning; she loved young people, but then again she encouraged smoking as well!

Pre-marital sex was the subject of a recent television documentary which explored the changing social habits of the last 75 years. Obviously the trials, uncertainties, and disruption of war had impacted heavily on otherwise 'acceptable' behaviour patterns, but it was extraordinary how so many of the older people interviewed – particularly the women – talked of the taboo and risk associated with pre-marital sex right up to the early 70s, when our relationship was testing values within both our families.

But what I found most disturbing in the documentary was the interview with a pair of teenage 'men' who challenged their grandparents' views on the merits of pre-marriage celibacy. 'Crazy' said one – 'why would you sign up without trying out the goods first?'. Such hard-nosed consumerism is, of course, common to most aspects of today's living, but even the most ardent supporters of consumer protection policies would hold that such attitudes are hardly applicable to the precious institution of marriage.

Many architects suffer similar problems when beginning relationships with prospective clients. Time and time again, clients are unhappy with references, past examples of work, even method statements and extended interviews. Instead, they want to see an indication of the architect's design response to their particular project, and therefore push to 'try out' the service before signing up. You know the line – 'we don't want much, just first ideas, just a simple sketch', all that nonsense.

As I have said before, try asking six barristers to set out their skeleton argument for a case in competition with each other – and for no pay. No chance! But architects seem ever willing and ever daft enough to give away their most precious skills for nothing. Often, they don't even pre-agree the appointment terms that they wish to apply if they are subsequently engaged.

When will clients learn that the design response to a particular site is dependent on the quality of brief, and on close collaboration between client and architect? Indeed, the more ambitious the client, the more complex the briefing process and the closer the collaboration that will be necessary. 'First responses' to a site have little value: design proposals should evolve through processes of testing and refinement and should be informed by carefully prepared design briefs.

And here we get to the real rub. Effective collaboration between architect and client cannot take place outside the parameters of a trusting relationship. Where an architect believes that a prospective client may freely take ideas from a variety of schemes, and 'mix and match' them – even pass them to his friendly design-and-build contractor – he is hardly likely to want to share them openly. And anyway, why should an architect invest such extensive time and skill without a fee commitment? We all know that when architects do provide such services freely, it is their staff who suffer. Furthermore, how can this profession maintain appropriate standards, and regain decent pay levels for its members, if it gives away its most valuable services for nothing?

Clearly, it seems to be a symptom of the age that 'consumers', be they patrons of architecture, or prospective marriage partners, all want to sample the goods before making any commitment. But such sampling doesn't seem to lead to better architecture or happier relationships between clients and their consultants, any more than it leads to happier or longer marriages. Indeed, divorces are at an all-time high, just as criticisms of architectural services and professional indemnity claims continue to rise.

I am not suggesting a return to conventional methods of professional selection any more than I am proposing a ban on pre-marital sex – and anyway neither are deliverable. But, just as with the selection of a 'life' partner, less greedy, less exploitative and more responsible selection processes would be fairer and better for all concerned.

Compulsory competitive tendering: a recipe for misery

The architectural profession clung blindly to the mandatory minimum fee scale some 25 years ago, even where the task of production information was largely transferred to specialist sub-contractors such as steel fabricators and cladders on industrial buildings. There were no concessions to 'front-loaded' fee scales, even on aborted projects.

Developers licked their wounds and harboured their grudges until commercially minded architects eventually broke rank in the face of huge changes in the development and construction industry. The mandatory minimum fee scale was finally scrapped when a pious institute was forced to introduce the 'recommended minimum fee scale' under which fees of course tumbled. To add to the agony, the high-tide of Thatcherism has now thundered through the doors of Portland Place in the form of Compulsory Competitive Tendering (author's note: happily this policy is now largely abandoned).

CCT really hurts yet cries for mercy go unheard and the RIBA's dignified and justified critique that CCT erodes the quality of service is lost on minds incapable of any decision that is not numerate. Describing CCT as a disease 'striking at the heart of British architecture . . . a recipe for second-rate buildings' Alex Reid, in a recent and well argued RIBA publication, sets out the case for public bodies to instead adopt the Brooks method of selection as used successfully in the USA .

This involves seven steps for clients: advertisement, submissions, assessment, quality ranking, interviews/discussions, negotiation and lastly engagement. After quality ranking, negotiation on appointment terms and fees commences with the top ranked firm, and only if agreement cannot be reached do negotiations begin with the second choice firm and so on, down the line until agreement is reached. The client has complete freedom to select the criteria used in compiling the shortlist, and the method ensures that the most appropriate architect is appointed at an acceptable price.

There is one absolute condition: failed negotiations must be terminated irrevocably before discussions open with alternative firms. This is a real test of an integrity which is fast vanishing across the entire development and construction industry.

I am reminded that some years ago a taxi-driver refused to slow down because my client had bartered too low a fare. Unprotected in that country by regulated charging rates the driver protested that he couldn't 'survive' unless he hurried dangerously and cut corners. Fearful for our lives my client agreed to pay more for a 'safe' ride of better quality.

There are parallels between that taxi ride and circumstances today under CCT. Quite simply, quality and fees cannot be considered in parallel, as the current CCT procedures intend, because economy of fees inevitably becomes the governing criteria in selection.

The RIBA is seeking general adoption of the Brooks method with the longer-term intention for its introduction into statute law for all Government projects – some hope! There is, however, a case for going even further and faster by introducing Institute obligations on all architects to refuse CCT. It may be unsavoury to some, but the RIBA can pursue self-interest through protectionist policies by calling a good old fashioned strike. But could we hold the line?

Keeping the lid on claims

Back in February 1999 I discussed a ruling by Mr Justice Dyson which affirmed that an architect who had stipulated a limit of £250,000 under clause 6.2 of the SFA/92 Memorandum of Agreement had satisfied the 'test of reasonableness' under Section 11 of the Unfair Contract Terms Act 1977 ('UCTA') and was therefore entitled to restrict the extent of his liability to that figure.

The client would not accept the decision, so the whole business subsequently dragged on to the Court of Appeal. On 23 March 2000, Lord Justices Beldam, Chadwick and Robert Walker upheld Mr Justice Dyson's decision. One of the reasons given was that when the contract between the architect and the client was made (which is the crucial date under UCTA for determining the effectiveness of a limitation of liability clause), the overall construction value of the project – a new house – had been estimated at about £225,000, and in that context the adoption of the £250,000 figure was deemed to have been rational as opposed to arbitrary. In previous decisions, the courts have struck down such limitation clauses because the amounts involved were deemed to have been set on an arbitrary basis.

As leave for further appeal to the House of Lords was refused, we can now be confident of our right to limit liability provided that the figure adopted can be shown to have been reasonable. This decision has very important implications for both architects and professional indemnity insurers, and Squire and Co, the lawyers who acted in this case, have clearly done both the profession and PI companies a great service.

Unfortunately, however, SFA/99 has now replaced the old SFA/92 clause 6.2 with an item under 'Articles of Agreement' that requires 'Limit of liability and amount of Professional Indemnity Insurance cover' to be stated. This implies that the figures are, or will be, the same which is misleading given that the architect may hold a higher level of PI cover than the figure that he is willing to accept as a limit of liability on any particular job. Indeed, Mr Justice Dyson had made it clear that while the level of an architect's insurance cover was a relevant factor to be taken into account, it was not the determining factor in deciding the reasonableness or otherwise of the limit of liability. PI cover is only one of a number of factors to be balanced against each other when making such an assessment.

Furthermore, disclosure of your PI details may breach your policy terms. So when using SFA/99 you should delete the words 'and amount of Professional Indemnity Insurance Cover' and simply ensure that you maintain cover at least to the stipulated level of liability plus a generous allowance to cover the other side's legal costs arising in any dispute.

One cheery bit of news is that a new clause has been added to SFA/99. Its true effect will have to be tested in the Courts, but the intention is clear enough: clause 9.6.1 obliges the client to 'indemnify' an architect with respect to 'legal and other costs' incurred, either when defending himself against an unsuccessful claim (or part claim), or in the successful pursuit of unpaid fees.

More interesting, however, is the provision within the same clause to the effect that the architect will, in such circumstances, be due a 'reasonable sum in respect of his own time spent in connection with such action or proceedings or any part thereof'. This provision will sure make trigger-happy clients think twice before commencing unwarranted actions – particularly when counter-claims are brought as a device for avoiding paying fees properly due. Bullying architects and their insurers into unfair 'settlements' by threatening enormous litigatiow costs is all too common. (One architect for whom I recently acted as expert Witness expended some £36,000 of professional time advising the PI litigation team during the successful defence of his case.)

Thanks to architect Stephen Yakeley, who introduced this clause into SFA/99, we can in future expect to be entitled to compensation when our personal time is wasted in this way. Hooray!

The dangers of late billing

Derry Irvine, in whose chambers Tony Blair and Cherry Booth both worked, published plans last year for major reforms to the legal aid system. The Lord Chancellor's strategy is two-pronged: firstly to extend 'conditional' no-win/no-fee arrangements to all civil proceedings except family cases, and secondly to reduce legal costs and make them more predictable through the introduction of streamlining procedures.

The burden of litigation to the taxpayer is indeed enormous. The annual costs of civil legal aid has tripled in six years to £671 million, while lawyers' income has risen on average by 20 per cent pa over the same period. Lawyers also earn enormous income through insurance work. One PI company has revealed that from £1 million of indemnity premiums received from architects, £800,000 was ultimately paid in legal fees for the investigation and defence of allegations made against their insured.

Many lawyers claim that 'conditional' fees will not provide for some cases that would otherwise receive legal aid, especially those with a low chance of success, because lawyers would not wish to accept the high risks involved. Many of these relate to construction disputes. Lord Irvine retorts bluntly that weak cases should be kept out of court anyway, adding that through legal aid 'lawyers draw almost at will for doing the work they choose to do'.

But I have considerable sympathy with the legal profession. The lawyers that I have worked with in construction litigation have consistently shown a high level of commitment to commercial pragmatism in the overall interests of their clients – whether individuals, companies, or insurers. Above all, they have shown the utmost integrity in pursuance of their client's interests, both when defending architects and occasionally in actions against them.

Nevertheless, the cost of litigation remains unacceptably high and construction/PI related litigation is no exception. That said, I think that nothing is gained by attacking the lawyers – rather, we should look at the legal system they operate and at the performance of the litigants that they represent, who are themselves often responsible for their own misfortunes.

Our legal profession could serve us with greater efficiency if a larger proportion of cases were dealt with through alternative routes which still involve the services of lawyers, albeit within a different and more economic system. I will look at a variety of alternative dispute resolution routes (ADRs) such as Mediation and Conciliation, Arbitration, and Adjudication over coming weeks.

However, the architect should, wherever possible, avoid disputes in the first place. By far the majority of cases that come to me as an expert witness are in the form of counter-claims by the client against an architect's action for unpaid fees. Using the 'right of offset', many clients try their luck with spurious allegations of negligence as a basis for withholding fees due. These cases usually involve lawyers in unavoidable, lengthy and expensive pre-trial rituals. By then, legal costs have often exceeded the value of the claim.

One simple solution would be for architects to refuse to issue practical completion certificates unless and until 95 per cent of their fees are paid. Most clients value such certificates, and linking them to efficient billing would effectively reduce the balance of outstanding fees to sufficiently small amounts not to warrant litigation. Now there's a dammed good thought . . .

Fees up front

'Please let me know if you would like some funds on account.' So concluded a letter of appointment last week from a new client. I was tempted to request £2,500 just like a solicitor would! But old habits die hard, and we decided to carry on our normal practice of trusting the integrity and decency of our clients by billing at intervals in arrears.

Events in recent weeks have illustrated the folly of such policy as the following story reveals. A commission late last year for alterations and extensions to a four-storey Victorian town house had been complicated by the requirement for a fast-track programme of urgent repairs. This we had arranged, letting a contract which was, to the credit of the builder, completed on time.

For no apparent reason, the client refused to pay our invoice, or the balance of money due to the builder. Our letters and phone calls unanswered, we are now taking legal action for fee recovery. All very irritating and very much an incentive to insist on payment in advance, especially for such relatively small sums.

But of course we all know the difficulty. 'Up-front' payments are normally nigh on impossible to negotiate for any job, small or large. Some other architect is always willing to give credit, if not substantially discounted fees, and honour between professionals is at a pretty low ebb with some offices seemingly ever on the look-out to poach work.

What a surprise, then, to receive a courteous letter from Mr Lipinski who wrote: '. . . I wish to notify you that I have been approached by Mr 'Z' (our dishonest client!) to organise further repairs and alterations . . . I should be most grateful if you would . . . confirm that your appointment has been terminated. This will enable me to decide whether or not I can accept the commission'.

On the strength of the low-down that I gave, I understand that Mr Lipinski has decided to save himself a lot of trouble by avoiding a very disreputable client. If more architects acted like Lipinski Pates, our profession would surely gain much greater respect from the many dishonest clients who mess architects around so badly.

Concurrent with these events we learned that another client – this time an Oxfordshire school – had passed our drawings on to a firm of 'architectural designers' who had offered some kind of cut-price deal to replace us. No matter that appointment terms had been agreed with us, and that we had completed a substantial package of work which is currently the subject of a grant application, and no matter that we have so far not been paid pending DfEE project approval. This, by the way, is not about competition or the quality of our performance, it's about unethical business behaviour and irresponsible clients.

None of Lipinski Pates' courtesy with this brazen outfit: no notification to us, no respect for copyright. They had cheekily added their title block to our drawings and proceeded on behalf of a client who should have known better than to allow this muddle to arise. With the threat of proceedings in respect of unpaid fees and breach of copyright we seem to be back on track, but it has been an unpleasant interlude.

Sadly, there is probably little that architects can do to protect themselves against such bad practice from hack 'design' companies, but we would certainly all do well to treat our own fellow professionals in the manner exemplified by Lipinski Pates.

Indeed obligations already exist under Paragraphs 3.4 and 3.8 of the RIBA Code of Conduct which bar us from attempting 'to oust another architect from an engagement' and oblige us to notify a fellow architect before supplanting him. However, the recently published new ARB Code of Conduct is conspicuously silent on such matters, despite their inclusion in the draft code which underwent consultation: I suppose that ARB have concluded that such courtesy amounts to a 'cronyism' over which even the most disreputable consumer's interests should prevail.

Messing with gangsters

'Paul, can you take your wife away for a while – find a lonely hotel somewhere, we'll pay . . .' This request, made some 20 years ago by a builder was, of course, met with bemused but firm refusal. He was distraught, but only later did I learn why, and in what danger I had also been. I'll change the names for obvious reasons, but essentially, the story goes like this . . .

Rexon Ltd, named after a greyhound racing dog that the company had once owned, had built their fortune as a labour-only sub-contractor, supplying unskilled men, very rough and ready, to main contractors for excavation, trench and foundation work.

They subsequently established their own construction company and got 'respectable' by persuading an accountant to join the board. Vic introduced a semblance of order into their chaotic administration, some planning into their growth, and some purpose into their investments and it was he who, with typical foresight, telephoned and begged me to leave town.

If I had known why, I would have surely gone, for I was the target of a gangland hit squad.

Donnelly, the company's founder, had always liked the drink and, despite being 'loyally' married, also the girls. Cruising home from a West End club through south-east London in the early hours of a Saturday morning, he had jumped a set of traffic lights. (He probably didn't even see them.)

His big Jaguar was in collision with a car driven by a well heeled lady journeying home from the night-club that she managed. Donnelly graduated that night into a hit-and-run driver: that much he vaguely remembered. What he didn't know was that he had done it in style. The woman that he left, seriously shaken but not stirred, was the moll of an underworld car dealer.

Radiator burst, blue paint streaked down the side of his green limousine, Donnelly struggled to his cousin's house where he habitually slept off his Friday night skinfull in the kitchen armchair.

It took the gangster's boys just four days to track him down. Vic received the call: 'I want the guy with the green Jag . . .' Donnelly instantly took off overseas, but Vic was made of sterner stuff and agreed to meet the gangster at one of Rexon's jobs. Unfortunately, my signboard was displayed at the site entrance.

The confrontation was awesome. Six cars blocked the street to through traffic, and two minders escorted the gangster in, only to learn from Vic that the man he wanted had done a bunk. That was when the threat against me was issued: 'I want that bastard, and if I don't get him I'll have the names on your hoarding out there'. Paul Hyett Architects was, regrettably, on the top – there were few aspiring project managers in those days.

Vic came of age through that confrontation – he did a deal that involved a new car, and a substantial cash payment. I was dropped from the 'wanted' list (albeit that it was some months before I learned that I had even been on it!) and, a nice touch this, the gangster subsequently gave Vic's firm some building work. No hard feelings!

The building industry is indeed a colourful world, mixing people of extraordinary backgrounds. I've met princes, politicians, the clever, the poor, the wealthy and the daft.

Once, at a charity dinner, a fellow guest bade me polite farewell. He had been appalled when I told him what trouble architects can have getting fees paid, and was wonderfully sympathetic and offered help when I explained the cost and delay involved in litigation.

'Who was he?' I later asked – he had been introduced as just Ernie. 'That', said my host, 'was Ernie Richardson'. For those of you too young to remember, he led one of the major rival gangs to the Krays in the 60's.

And a charming man he was too – I was minded to ask him to help me collect some of my bad debts . . .

The pitfalls of design-and-build

Design-and-build emerged in its present form when architects and quantity surveyors began to 'parcel up' elements of modern building construction and pass the task of detailed design on to specialist sub-contractors. (Typical examples were the steel frames and cladding of industrial sheds, and curtain-walling in office developments.)

Its use was further encouraged by the rapidly escalating cost of financing projects particularly during periods of high inflation. In such circumstances developers are obliged to delay all expenditure (site acquisition and professional fees) at least until they are certain that a project will proceed. Severe inflation, which peaked at over twenty-four percent in 1975 and again at eighteen percent in 1985, exerted intense pressure. As a consequence the construction of buildings was, with increasing frequency, begun without sufficient information and this led to ever more serious 'claims' arising from contractors against the late issue of instructions by the design team.

It was in order to protect against such claims that the quantity surveyors and developers looked to the benefits of design-and-build contracting (a process which could more accurately be described as detail-and-build). By procuring full d&b services against a written brief, or outline sketch, it eventually became possible to divert all responsibility for detailed design work (and delays consequent on the late supply of information) away from the client's professional team. However the contractor's role in this field is demanding, risk-laden, and poorly rewarded so why do they do it?

On paper, contracting is not very profitable and looks like an unattractive business. However, it does generate a positive cash flow very early in the building process, in the form of payments for work which are received before the sub-contractors and others who are responsible for executing that work have been paid.

As a typical example, one major contractor in 1990 maintained a positive balance of £200 million of certified monies against construction work in hand. To borrow such an amount would have cost some £30 million a year at interest rates of fifteen percent (the sort of preferential rates a big business could then expect). It is therefore well worth running a low profit (or even unprofitable) contracting business in order to obtain what is in effect a huge interest-free loan which can be used to fund other activities such as the acquisition of land, quarrying and property development.

The d&b contract not only reduces the role of the architect but it removes the traditional obstacles to the contractor's early application for money. It also improves the contractor's cash flow. Clearly, the interests of the developer and the contractors are closely aligned in this respect, and those interests have little to do with social concerns or with the aesthetic qualities of the built environment. Rather than serving the nation, the contracting industry has created the converse situation – one where the population serves the industry by unwittingly supplying it with large sums of money through the uncensured supply of pension and general investment funds.

There are, of course, distinct advantages in the design-and-build process but until we imbue the contracting industry with a broader remit of concern, the full advantages of these procedures will be constrained by the unduly narrow objectives of the majority of those involved.

Showdown in the saloon bar

Exasperated by the continuing failure of my client to respond to my letters demanding payment, I decided late one evening to go and see him. It's some twenty years ago now, but I remember it all well.

A publican in the Old Kent Road had run into trouble with the district surveyor over 'alterations' and drawings had been needed 'a bit quick'. Confirming my appointment in writing (strictly in line with the ARB's current requirements) I did the work and then sent in my bill with a polite covering note.

No joy. Polite reminder . . . Still no joy . . . And so it went on for over a year. The amount was not large but it was good money and it was rightly mine. Professional training and my new Part III qualification counted for nothing in this situation: the more I wrote, the less serious this character thought I was about getting paid. We talked a different language.

Anyway, looking bleakly with my wife at a list of outstanding debtors this particular evening I got angry – as I should have done months before – and set off for a showdown. Leaving my old Volkswagon under the sodium glare of a street lamp I walked purposefully into the pub. There, pouring a 'chaser' with his back to me, was my client. A hush descended over the room as I made my way – an obvious stranger – to the bar.

'That geezer wants a word,' murmured the bar girl pointing in my direction. The landlord strolled over but genuinely couldn't remember who I was. His face was a complete blank. Finally, he remembered. Bemused rather than outraged that I should press him publicly for cash (I was now talking his language) he suggested we 'go out the back to sort this out'. There, in the presence of his irritable Alsatian and his disinterested wife we argued . . .

He hadn't understood the fee basis, said I couldn't be serious about the money, and thought the bill was 'plain daft'. I complained bitterly that he hadn't answered my letters and insisted on payment. He said I was 'some kind of a nut'. Of course we were chalk and cheese – the aspiring professional and the streetwise rogue. Principle and integrity versus a wheeler-dealer on the make.

I quickly realised that this dispute was all my fault – I had played it wrong from the start, misjudging the man and failing to communicate in a way that he understood. He hadn't wanted an appointment letter – why should he? He'd never had one before and he had wanted a written invoice even less. His world was made up of bartered deals and rough but firm handshakes. It had its own rules and honour but it was a world away from anything I had been trained for. Part III had said nothing about this lot.

But, somehow, this tough diamond warmed to me. He obviously respected 'the visit' and the face to face exchange. 'Tell you what,' he eventually said – 'you can have all the money in the machines – how's that?'. (He meant the one-armed bandits). He grinned slyly and said they would 'more 'n likely cover you'.

Returning to the bar I held open several bags as coins were poured in, then refusing a drink, I quickly repaired to the car, and made a speedy getaway. My wife counted up later: I was just a few pounds short, but a good deal rougher and tougher myself.

Some time after, Danny asked me to do a job on his new house. I didn't bother with a written appointment and I never sent any bills – why should I? For his part, he paid on demand – but I always had to collect!

The next time I heard him mentioned, he had been shot dead in a gun-fight at the pub. Obviously, someone hadn't found him as straightforward to deal with as me! Pity really – I liked Danny.

Shotgun wedding

Much confusion still surrounds design-and-build procurement – its strengths are not sufficiently recognised or utilised by clients and it is usually used in such a bastardised form that it fails to function as design-and-build anyway. This is the main reason why its market share has peaked at only 23 per cent.

D&b's main benefits are single-point responsibility, early price commitment, and transfer of risk, but most clients seem to want to have their cake and eat it! They choose and use an architect for the early design work, and then try to pass him over to the builder. As a result, over 50 per cent of all d&b contracts are now tendered with novation of the architect/engineer as a pre-condition of appointment.

Novation not only means that the client's architect (chosen for his empathy with the client's interests) must, chameleon-like, become the contractor's man, but also that all the early services that he has already carried out for the client are 'novated' with him. Effectively the parties re-write history and pretend that all the pre-contract design work was supplied through the contractor, and not directly for the client. Thought up as an expediency by the QS profession, it is of course unfair to transfer responsibility for such work, which is after all outside the contractor's discipline, into his contract. However, the lean state of the industry has, in recent years, weakened its resolve to object to such conditions. As a consequence this ludicrous procedure is one of the major causes of the problems which discredit d&b.

The contractor understandably objects to the shot-gun marriage of novation. Most architects have difficulty changing sides, and the domination of the market by novation prevents contractors from developing in-house resources and skills. Finally, novation prevents d&b contractors from making a design contribution within their tenders because they are denied access to the architect until post-tender stage. By then the opportunity to benefit from close collaboration in design development between architect and contractor has usually been lost.

A further 20 per cent of the d&b sector is 'develop and construct' – not considered to be d&b at all as the design and specification are fairly complete at tender. Here, the contractor is simply being asked to take on more liability by agreeing to fix his price and 'cover any gaps' in the construction information.

This leaves something like 25 per cent of the d&b sector as the real thing, where the client approaches the design contractor with a brief only. In this scenario the skilled d&b contractor – one with competent designers and good experience of similar projects – is able to provide the client at an early stage with the full range of advice on the building and site, the budget and the programme. Unfortunately most d&b contractors who are effective in this field can only cope with repetitive and relatively simple building types within the fields of industrial, commercial and housebuilding work. That said, some, such as Pearce Construction, have developed a capacity to deliver highly specialised and sophisticated buildings through their d&b division.

Only where clients learn to use d&b properly can it be an effective route for procurement. However, when the client is in a position to provide a clear brief for a building project, and if the context is relatively simple – for example a clear site and no planning difficulties – design-and-build has a real role to play, provided of course that a good contractor is chosen.

Copywrong – the d&b nightmare

'Copywrong', the antithesis of copyright, has emerged as a significant threat to both architects and architecture in recent years. Initiatives to curtail this miserably corrupting process are long overdue and it's high time our profession woke up and took some action. Why has this crisis emerged so suddenly, and who is responsible?

'Copywrong', (yet to find its way into the Oxford Dictionary), is the ugly by-product of the arrogant and irresponsible meddling with the processes of building procurement that have become the hallmarks of the hack-end of the construction industry.

'Copywrong' involves the wresting of a design concept from its author following inception, the thoughtless violation of that proposal during working drawing stage, and the further sabotaging of design intent during construction.

'Copywrong' occurs when a quality project is taken from the concept designers and handed to hacks for onward development, usually within the design-and-build process.

'Copywrong' continues when wretched building managers interfere and further damage an architecture during its construction.

Three recently I have been approached by major architects distraught about the consequences of 'copywrong'. Sidelined by the developer's decision to appoint a d&b company following receipt of planning permission, one architect watched helpless as his work was corrupted during its development. His anguish deepened when he saw the results of the so-called project manager's further interference with the design during 'co-ordination' of the production information.

It is of the utmost importance that architects are protected from such wretched abuse. It is potentially devastating for their reputations, and has adverse implications for those who ultimately use the buildings. Indeed, we rely heavily on our built work to enhance our reputation, and successful projects are essential to the securing of new commissions. Where the products of our imagination are corrupted during gestation and delivery, our interests are threatened.

Of course, in the days when architects were routinely appointed for the entire duration of a project – from sketch stage to handover (RIBA Stages C-L) – 'copywrong' used to be relatively rare. In these circumstances the architect was able to develop and refine his design concepts through the working drawing stage, and through his authority he could safeguard design integrity during construction.

All that is now threatened with increasing and grim regularity by the incessant, and sadly all too frequent successful attempts of others (be they quantity surveyors, project managers or contractors), to hijack procurement processes and compromise design objectives in order to satisfy their rude agendas.

Weneed to address these problems by finding new ways of improving modern procurement processes – calls for the exclusive return to traditional appointments will find little favour, and indeed they shouldn't.

But such new ways must involve a concerted willingness by others to resolve problems of 'copywrong'. Government, clients, and the growing numbers of naive and ignorant champions of the cheap and tacky, who have gained so much influence in the quantity surveying and contracting companies, must all wake up to their responsibilities in this respect.

Only by maintaining their skill and knowledge in the processes of construction can architects who wish to build resist the 'copywrong' which is the cause of so much of the 'architackiness' that surrounds us. Meanwhile, how long until some architect launches the first legal claim for damages arising from 'copywrong'?

Getting tough over unpaid bills

It is a disturbing fact that a large proportion of legal disputes between architects and their clients take the form of a counter-claim for negligence in response to legal action for outstanding fees.

As an expert witness I see an all too familiar story particularly on smaller jobs: the architect has struggled to bring the work to a conclusion, practical completion draws near and snagging lists are prepared. The client, by now exhausted and intolerant of the processes of the construction industry, is issued with a proportionately large invoice – frequently as much as 30 per cent of the overall fee payable to the architect due to late billing. The account remains unpaid and, exasperated, the architect eventually sues.

By this time, of course, the client has got what he wants: the building has been handed over, practical completion certificates have been issued, and the architect has little left to offer.

The antidote to such misfortune is to bill regularly, never extending credit far, and to ensure that fees are paid up to date, and well before the project 'handover', while the client is still heavily dependent on the architect's services. If on completion the architect was due, say, only 5 per cent of his fee, most disputes would never proceed to litigation as the small amounts involved would not warrant the risks of expensive legal fees – on either side.

Professionals in the construction industry all invoice in arrears, and in recent decades, with the introduction of increased competition and a substantial proportion of speculative work, the time lag between doing work, billing and eventual receipt of payment has extended enormously. Among consultants, architects have suffered particularly heavily in this respect. By contrast, the medical profession is largely assured payment through the State as a third party, and lawyers frequently demand fees on account and, with their accountancy friends, readily suspend or withdraw services when payments are not made promptly. Architects are very nervous of such action.

I recently proposed that Insurers should impose conditions for PI cover that require a prescribed proportion (say 95 per cent of all fees due to that stage) to be paid to the architect before a Practical Completion Certificate could be issued. Failure to procure such payment would incur breach of insurance conditions rendering the architect's policy void – no client wants that! Such a condition would of course ensure that most clients, particularly developers, pay willingly: practical completion certificates are an important part of property letting and sale procedures, especially to investment companies.

Under the intense pressure of competition, architects would, however, never unilaterally impose such conditions and the RIBA is sadly too weak to enforce them. It's a move that only the PI companies could initiate.

Surprisingly, this proposal does not interest insurers, despite significant potential reductions in PI claims. They too must compete for business and any such conditions are deemed unattractive to the insurance market. With the insurers unwilling to impose obligations to bill early, and with architects apparently unable to muster such will, a high level of claims that are consequential on late billing will continue (lucky lawyers!).

That is unless, of course, more architects sharpen up and invoice regularly, withholding later valuable certificates through which they substantially extend their responsibilities, until they are properly paid. Such firm action would save both heartache and the heavy financial costs of litigation.

A VAT sting

Here's a story regarding VAT with big implications for architects who settle a fee dispute outside Court – that is, after issuing proceedings but before judgement.

Essentially, it means that where you accept a lesser sum (which might, I guess, be as much as 99.9 per cent of the full amount claimed) you and your client may argue that the payment is VAT-exempt. This is not a 'ruse'; it is based on a judgement in *Reich* v *The Commissioners of Customs and Excise* which was heard at no less an authority than the Manchester VAT tribunal in December 1992.

The facts: The Appellant worked as a merger broker and in that capacity he charged fees on a commission basis – either against the vendor, the purchaser, or partly against each. Commission had been charged from travel company Hogg Robinson relating to work that had involved research, information and an introduction to a firm owning 'travel shops' (offering holiday package tours) that were to be sold.

Having obtained agreement to his fee proposal, and after providing the services mentioned, the appellant received a letter from Hogg Robinson advising that they wished to proceed no further with the purchase. Later, the appellant learned that his ex-client had, however, proceeded to acquire the 'travel shops' without further contacting him. (This story is all too familiar to those architects who have been 'shafted' by developer clients.)

Hogg Robinson refused to pay and litigation was commenced by the appellant for £45,000 plus costs. VAT was applicable on top of this figure. However, after a good round of haggling an offer of £35,000, inclusive of all costs, was accepted at the court doors 'in full and final settlement'.

That sum was duly paid and banked by the appellant but, later, VAT officers noted that no VAT had been charged on the sum. They subsequently brought an action for VAT at the standard rate on the £35,000 which they alleged was a part payment against the £45,000 fee (net of VAT) billed to Hobb Robinson. Surprisingly, the Manchester Tribunal found in favour of the appellant – ie that no VAT was chargeable. So what logic supported this decision?

Firstly, the tribunal decided that although VAT would be chargeable where a taxpayer sues and recovers judgement for an amount of an invoice on which VAT is properly applicable 'as being in respect of a supply', it is quite another situation where judgement has not been obtained. (This case was, remember, settled before judgement.) Hogg Robinson had never admitted that a taxable supply had been received: they had merely made a payment to avoid the embarrassment, cost and risk of a trial.

The tribunal deemed that it must be apparent that something has been done, as well as done for a consideration, in order to give rise to a taxable supply as stipulated under Section 3(2)(b) of the VAT Act 1983!

Apparently, sums received by way of settlement of litigation, such as in this case, represent 'consideration' of a complex nature. What element of legal costs are included? What element of a payment which is 'in full and final settlement' relates to embarrassment that a Defendant would otherwise cause to a plaintiff, financial or otherwise, in pursuing a claim? In conclusion, the tribunal decided that the parties in the case outlined above had placed on the claim an agreed estimate of its worth as a claim, not because they recognised that consideration was being paid for a supply that had been made, or for the transfer of any benefit such as copyright.

The appeal against the Customs and Excise demand for VAT on the settlement figure was therefore successful.

But as TV star Davina says – 'Don't try this yourself'. And don't conspire to defraud – you must not collude with a client to construct a false dispute and 'settlement' – that would be very naughty! As Robert Hogarth, of solicitors Reynolds Porter Chamberlain (who provided me with this intriguing story) says: you should always ensure proper legal and accounting advice in any similar circumstances.

Design & VAT

Tim Gough's letter (AJ 10.7.97) draws attention to an important aspect of VAT legislation which encourages the adoption of design-and-build as a procurement route in order to save VAT on professional fees.

Those who are not VAT-registered, and who therefore have no mechanism for reclaiming VAT paid for professional services, may use d&b to exploit an anomaly which renders professional fees eligible for VAT even on jobs where the construction work is zero-rated. Under design-and-build, the builder pays the architect, reclaims the VAT and issues an overall zero-rated account to the client. Architects are severely disadvantaged by this legislation.

VAT legislation is complex, onerous and inconsistent. For example, some building types are zero-rated, such as new-build private dwellings; relevant residential uses such as prisons, elderly persons' homes, hospices, school accommodation, drug and alcohol rehabilitation facilities; and even 'monasteries convents or similar places'. Presumably therefore a Buddhist retreat qualifies, but why a hospice and not a hospital?

Listed-building 'alterations' qualify for zero-rating but their maintenance and repair carries VAT at the standard rate. What is an alteration? We might consider a new roof comprising vapour barriers and thermal insulation in lieu of simple slate on batten to be an alteration – the VAT office takes more persuasion

Recent years have seen major shifts in VAT legislation. VAT was zero-rated on all new construction until April 1989, when it became applicable to a wide category of new-build work. Extensions were zero-rated until 1984 but then became subject to the standard charge.

Efforts were made in March 1995 to better define the word 'extension', a term that had bedevilled customs officers. Accordingly, the adding of an extension building of normally zero-rated category may now attract VAT unless the new accommodation 'stands alone' in terms of facilities such as separate entrance, WCs, boiler rooms etc. Avoiding VAT by delaying construction of a linking 'corridor' until a later building contract can be dangerous: powers exist to levy VAT retrospectively and charges of tax avoidance or evasion are possible.

Architects who try to help their clients in such situations should be very careful as errors leading to later claims by Customs and Excise may lead to litigation.

Brian Davis of accountant Saffery Champness has developed a specialism in this field. He can make an invaluable contribution at the early design stage where certainty of VAT application is critical to the project's viability. In one case a new residential building was being constructed behind a retained facade, the retention being a requirement of the planners but not the developer who wanted, on the one hand, a completely new building, and, on the other, a project of zero-rated VAT. Brian was able to negotiate with the VAT office and gain a favourable ruling early in the project, thus providing the certainty which was an essential prerequisite to the job proceeding.

His role can also usefully extend to advising on design arrangements which optimise the VAT situation. Valuable as this service undoubtedly is, many will be highly critical of a taxation system that directly affects design outcomes.

I commend architects to treat this area with great caution. Establish the VAT categorisation of your project early, and involve experts in complex situations. If you give advice that is wrong, any subsequent claim that the subject was outside your expertise, especially complex, or that you were merely just 'trying to help' will hardly protect you from a PI negligence claim.

VATMAN threatens practice

David Rock is absolutely right to press home his case against VAT anomalies favouring design-and-build - as reported in the AJ last week.

Initially prompted to action by this column (AJ 3.7.97 and 21.8.97), and questions by Tim Gough (AJ letters 10.7.97), Rock wrote to arts minister Mark Fisher in October. No stranger to the world of architecture, Fisher was co-author of 'A New London' with Richard Rogers. But does he – can he – understand the relationship between architectural process and product? Evidently not, despite his long and close association with Lord R.

His response to David Rock offers nothing. Instead of reviewing this unsatisfactory situation, he stubbornly claims that the 'right course must surely be to encourage good design quality in design-build projects rather than condemning the approach which some customers clearly want'. He misses the point.

The difficulties that both architects and clients face due to this ridiculous VAT anomaly was again highlighted only yesterday by accountants Saffery Champness who offer specialist advice in construction related VAT. A charity appointed an architect for a £5 million job, incurring VAT of £44,000 on the firm's fees – a substantial tax which (and this is the key point) this charity cannot reclaim because they are not VAT registered.

Faced with these circumstances they are being forced – completely contrary to what Mr Fisher says – to do exactly the opposite of what they 'clearly want'. Come on Mr Fisher this is silly! The VAT is completely avoidable if this charity appoints an untrained builder to design their work, but they must pay an enormous sum in VAT if they directly appoint a professional, qualified and registered architect (ARB this is also about protecting consumer interests – you can't stay silent on this one!)

'Ah!' some may say – 'why not novate the architect?' This doesn't work. If the client novates early he is saddled with a builder before he has a competitive tender or a design. If he novates late, all fees payable up to the time of novation are subject to VAT.

I am a strong advocate of d&b when done properly. Again I refer to Pearce Construction who are leaders in this field applying considerable management skills to a process which they are committed to, understand, and properly resource. But this is an option that works effectively in the commercial field where the client's decision to opt for a d&b procurement route is based on its appropriateness to the project needs – not some silly loophole in the VAT legislation.

We expect more from government in the interests of choice for consumers: they should be able to adopt the traditional appointment route for this kind of work if they prefer without the penalty of VAT. We also expect greater fairness for the architect: our profession should not be disadvantaged at selection stage by daft taxation anomalies.

We need this anomaly removed – without further procrastination – in the interests of good design, which is always dependent on process. A client must be free to select and manage the team and procurement route of his choice without unfair tax penalties. We won't give up on this one. . .

PART 3

Managing the office

Standing up for staff

The great thing about the recent *Munkenbeck & Marshall* v *Kensington Hotel* case is that Judge Wilcox has endorsed what everybody in our profession already knows – everybody, that is, except the ARB: you don't need to be a registered architect to design good buildings! A fuller account of this litigation is given by Kim Franklyn in this week's Journal, but let us here consider some of its wider implications.

While stating that under UK law those who provide architectural services are not entitled to call themselves architects unless they are registered, Wilcox revealed the essential flaw that renders the Registration Act absurd and futile when he said: 'There is no prohibition, however, against carrying out architectural work'.

We all know that despite not being registered, Zaha Hadid is held in the highest esteem around the world. Yet she could be hauled into court for calling herself an architect – if, that is, the ARB would ever dare! Why do we continue with this nonsense whereby the term architect is legally denied to some of our best architects? Protection of title remains a farce!

Check out the status of our leading teachers – SCHOSA (Standing Conference of Heads of Schools of Architecture) is increasingly attended by delegates who are not 'architects'. Helen Mallinson, Colin Stansfield Smith's deputy on the RIBA committee currently reviewing of education and Head of the North London school is not registered, nor is Portsmouth head Wendy Potts. Peter Salter, like Zaha, one of the outstanding architects of his generation and now head of East London, cannot use the title either, and there are many others . . .

In saying that our Part III exam deals with matters of project and practice management, the judge went on to draw a fascinating distinction which most architects also accept. In concluding that Munkenbeck & Marshall's engagement had not required 'any of the skills falling within Part III' – despite having 'involved the preparation of design . . . tender and construction' drawings, the judge affirmed that it is possible to carry out such work without having a Part III qualification – again something everybody accepts – except the ARB!

In assessing the status and quality of Munkenbeck & Marshall staff who were unregistered, the judge was satisfied that they 'were of high standard by academic qualification and practical experience', and that their pay should reflect that fact. Accordingly the judge found that the firm had been justified in charging out the time of their senior 'assistants' at the market rate for registered architects!

This conclusion has wide implications which will hopefully benefit those unqualified and underpaid staff across this country who are so disadvantaged by the consequences of the Registration Act.

The client had argued that rates of only £15 an hour for such staff were applicable. After normal allowances for profit and overheads this racks back to £5 an hour salary – or £8,700 a year before tax, which is a disgrace after only three years in university education let alone five years at college and several more in practice!

Brian Green, chairman of GML Architects, should be ashamed of himself for arguing in court that such rates were 'fair and reasonable'. The judge, preferring the evidence of Peter Melvin, admonished Green severely, saying that he had lost sight of the role of an expert witness.

But the final, and for me delicious, irony in this case was that this tight-fisted client was represented by Mischon De Reya, about whom I have previously written (AJ 18.3.99). Remember them? They were reported as charging over £2.3 million as solicitors to Princess Diana's Memorial Fund. If Alfred Munkenbeck were to apply his charging rate, as allowed by Judge Wilcox, to Mischon de Reya's £2.3 million bill, it would take him 57,500 hours to earn the fee – that is full time until the year 2033, when Alf will be 83 years old!

In courageously fighting this case, Munkenbeck has at last proved that architects and architecture have real commercial value which should be properly respected and paid for. He should be heartily applauded.

Everyone needs a Samantha

The East Midlands Region (one of the 14 regions of the RIBA) has begun a system of 'practice visits' – a dull title that understates this innovative venture.

It started like this: Samantha Bramley, the regional administrator, decided with her boss to convert her role from a 'reactive' office-based operation to 'pro-active' mode. With their regional council, they persuaded Alex Reid at HQ to support a trial period wherein she would visit – yes go and visit – each and every RIBA registered practice in their region.

This service is free and these practice visits have been a resounding success, providing an initiative now available for all other regions to adopt, tailored as they require, to their own circumstances. Northern Region is already developing its own proposals for a similar service.

So what is a practice visit? Ever curious, I persuaded Samantha to venture south to give our office the standard 'Eastern Treatment'. We were amazed!

Arriving in a smart green suit with a beaming smile, Samantha brings a lap-top PC and a big sense of humour. Her no-nonsense presentation is well structured and efficiently delivered, breaking into four parts comprising updates on: branch news, contract and publications, RIBA services and Ribanet information.

Able to adapt the three-hour session to suit the small single practitioner on the one hand, or the large commercial office on the other, Samantha provides an invaluable audit/health-check on practice information sources and operations on an annual basis – and its all so orderly and so easy. Although not an architect herself, she has an extraordinary empathy with our profession and a gutsy working knowledge of our administrative systems and managerial needs.

Every practice needs a 'Samantha' – we're hooked and commend these visits wholeheartedly. Indeed if our London region doesn't set up an equivalent service by next year we'll simply join East Midland region instead!

We received a wealth of information including advice on updates to building contracts, developments with SFAs, and an introduction to the latest yellow guideline publications. She carries samples of all these – jokingly describing herself as the RIBA hostess with a goodies trolley – and willingly offers trial runs on the various RIBA pc offerings. She is also a mine of information on anticipated publications and amendments to building legislation.

The shocking truth for us was that Samantha's visit revealed important gaps. We simply didn't have, or even know about, some of the latest contract amendments, and I was unaware of a series of new information 'packs' now available on disc – for example CAFGEN which allows offices to produce, from their own pc, all their standard contract administration forms (practical completion certificates, interim payment certificates, routine notices and architect's instructions), eliminating the need to order printed forms from RIBA Publications.

East Midland members can ring or e-mail Samantha for further help during the year. Her service is simply superb and the East Midland region should be commended for their enterprise and initiative. It has, of course, realised that the stream of RIBA circulars routinely issued to members is not being absorbed, and that the introduction of a personal review is an effective and much needed means of communication and support for practices.

The tax time-bomb

'Employment status is not a matter of choice. Parties cannot simply decide to treat working arrangements as either self-employment or employment. The circumstances of the engagement determine how it is to be treated.'

This quotation is taken directly from the Inland Revenue's publication 'Employed or self-employed?' Employees should take careful heed. Employers who breech it do so at their peril: the penalties are draconian. A firm employing ten staff on a self-employed basis of £20,000 a year each could face a £360,000 demand for back payment of tax and National Insurance contributions if the Revenue's criteria for Schedule D status is not strictly complied with. That alone is enough to bankrupt most smaller firms, but worse still, penalties of up to 100 per cent of due payments can be levied as a further surcharge on repeat offenders.

In 'status-disputes' (that is a Revenue review to validate self-employment in lieu of PAYE Schedule E status) an inspector will make a ruling on a disputed Revenue Auditor's decision. Thereafter, appeal to a commissioner is possible, but it is usually a downhill ride to enforcement – with interest running on all unpaid sums.

The employer and the employee are both liable for any shortfall in taxation returns – but the Revenue usually demands payment from the employer. The method of recovery can be fearsome: the Revenue is entitled to recover all PAYE and DHSS payments that would have been payable directly from the employer, subsequently giving refunds to the employee of any contributions previously made under self-employed status.

Often tipped-off anonymously, occasionally investigating irregular tax returns, otherwise merely performing routine checks (expect at least one every five or six years and they are becoming more frequent) the Revenue's auditor has the power to access all material information, and can demand immediate payment of any monies due. Warnings were issued to the construction industry some nine months ago to clean up the alleged abuses of Schedule D categorisation. That expired on April 6 this year and the whips are now out. Professionals would be fools to consider themselves exempt.

The recent growth in self-employed status has, of course, been encouraged by changes in the marketplace and advances in communication technologies (distance working by computer/improved communications etc). 'Outsourcing,' says Jon Young, head of human resources at accountant Saffery Champness 'is a trend for modern service providers, especially where they face rapid fluctuations in supply demands, and for specialisms which are not always needed' (eg a perspective artist). However, the stark truth is that taxation law and procedures are lagging behind the tide of change.

Firms who fail to recognise the dangers of breaching current legislation – however intransigent and inappropriate taxation law may appear – are courting disaster. Remember, as professionals without limited liability employers are personally liable for their taxation errors.

Employers should ensure that only self-employed contract arrangements that comply with sound accountancy advice are continued. Otherwise, you leave a time bomb under your firm that could explode at any moment.

Exploitation of salaried staff

This is a true and cautionary tale which serves as a severe indictment of the malpractices of one of our leading architects. Sadly, it is also a common story that indicates both a deterioration in employment conditions generally and, in particular, a growing irresponsibility and selfishness among many architects as employers.

A young architect was invited to join a renowned practice needing help with a competition. He was seduced by a dazzling offer: to substitute his current proper job (PAYE, formal employment conditions etc) for a chance to work with a star. The opportunity brought no practical reward, only hope. No pay, no formal contract, no sickness benefit, nothing. On offer only a promise – success in the competition would bring the possibility of subsequent paid work. Future employment conditions, however, remained ominously undisclosed.

Worse was to come. The offer was conditional upon him starting immediately, thus breaching his existing contract through failing to work his notice. Irresponsibly, and at great inconvenience to his old firm, he gathered his pens and left that Friday.

Tuesday morning, and tearful, he was back – distraught that he had been made 'redundant' on his first day. The new boss had miscalculated his requirements and three naive young hacks had turned up when only two were needed! Our friend wanted sympathy, advice and his job back. He got the first two.

Similar circumstances are all too common. I know of one unscrupulous commercial office which staffed an entire division working on speculative projects almost wholly from 'unemployed' architects. Unpaid, with no employment contract, some drew dole and all worked on the premise that they would receive first consideration for opportunities arising if their speculative job converted to real. Such arrangements are immoral, illegal and ill-judged. They do untold damage to the profession: plundering its resource and diminishing its image in the eyes of clients.

The last government's pursuit of 'flexibility' within the workforce, apparently at almost any cost, has of course encouraged such initiatives.

The high levels of unemployment consequent upon the recession and property market collapse have worsened the situation, but that is no excuse: bad practices are bad practises whatever the cause. Such ruthless employers – no matter how great their so-called stardom – should be brought to book.

Sadly, the RIBA and ARB appear powerless. The RIBA gives guidance on salaries, no more. It cannot in practical terms impose employment conditions, but perhaps with ARB it should establish approved standards of conduct among architect employers as a basic condition for membership. The best way forward is, however, for employees to develop and enforce their own checklist of conditions, and for major client groups to take an exemplary lead by insisting on minimal acceptable working conditions for staff within commissioned firms

This week begins a new period whereby the country has placed its faith in a government that appears to subscribe to individual creativity, while endorsing social justice as a respectable objective. It's high time many architects did the same.

Just what is self-employed status?

A common response during Inland Revenue status investigations is: 'We've got no written contract so the person must be self-employed.'

This is a useless defence. The Inland Revenue's criterion is that where a person works in return for payment, 'a contract must exist'. This contract can be written, spoken, implied or a combination of all three. So, what are the criteria used for assessment?

Solicitor Steven Lorber, of Field Fisher Waterhouse, specialises in this area and says that there is no statutory definition of 'employment' for income tax purposes. Various reported cases provide guidance on distinguishing employment from self-employment, but no factor has been identified as the sole determinant – nor has an exhaustive list of characteristics been identified. He suggests the following test question should be applied to each case: 'Is the person engaged to perform these services performing them on his/her own account?' If the answer is yes, there is self-employment (a contract for services).If no, there is employment (a contract of service).

The Inland Revenue lists the following points, which are amplified in its publication 'Employed or self-employed?' (Any one, or a combination of some or all, may determine any particular case):

● Right of control: The degree of direction or control a contractor has over the worker – the greater the degree of control, the more probable it is that the worker is an employee. Who has control over what is to be done, when, and how?

● Equipment: If workers use the contractor's equipment (drawing boards, CAD, telephones etc), this suggests employment.

● Risk: The self-employed worker should be exposed to a risk of financial loss.

● Payment terms: Fixed hourly rates, or weekly/monthly regular payments, suggests employment. Lump-sum agreements for completion of defined tasks suggests self-employment.

● Substitution: The right of the worker to hire and pay someone else to take his/her place suggests self-employment.

● Length of engagement: This may also be a factor. Long terms of engagement will be typical of employment, but even very short-term engagements can amount to employment. Regular working for the same contractor (even under daily or weekly contracts) points towards employment.

● Benefits: Rights to benefits such as holidays, or statutory sick pay, are of decreasing importance as indicators due to the general deterioration in employment conditions over recent years.

Other relevant matters for consideration would include whether the worker incurs expenditure on his/her account, and whether the work/contract was won by the worker as a result of a competitive tendering process.

As Tim Gough kindly pointed out in his letter (AJ 15.5.97), the proper recording of terms of employment with respect to 'scope of services, responsibilities, remuneration, and provision for termination' is an obligation for all architects (employers and employees) under the new RIBA and ARB codes of conduct. In other words, failure to record employment terms will be a breach of professional duty which may result in disciplinary action from both the institute and registration board. The screw will thus tighten further, since a written contract, as required under the respective codes of conduct, will provide explicit evidence of status with reference to Schedule D (self-employed) and Schedule E (PAYE) Inland Revenue assessments. You have been warned!

Tax dodgers hurt us all

Over recent weeks I have outlined the Inland Revenue's criteria for assessing self-employed or PAYE status, warning of the dangers arising through taxation rule breaches. (The financial penalties can be very severe - see AJ 22.5.97 and 29.5.97).

Offices who dodge tax by wrongly contracting staff on a self-employed basis (among which are disgracefully included some star names) often incite PAYE status workers to breach taxation legislation by only offering Schedule D contract terms (there appear to be ever fewer PAYE jobs around!).

Through such policy 'tax dodging', offices can reduce wage bills by up to 30 per cent. This 'saving' is reflected in reduced fees – labour costs usually constitute between 40 and 50 per cent of office turnover, so offices that avoid PAYE where it is properly due effectively reduce operational costs by some 12 to 15 per cent. This enables them to slash fees as they invariably pass the savings on to their clients. These firms thus operate at a distinct advantage over offices that properly apply the Inland Revenue's taxation laws - they therefore win more work through cheaper fee bids. The 'pitch' for competition between practices is thus uneven – something of great current importance as so much architectural work is nowadays awarded on a cost/fee criteria, often through competitive tendering.

Workers have a moral responsibility in this respect. They should not permit bosses to abuse their professional interests and misapply their talents. By wrongly accepting or adopting Schedule D status, workers act against their salaried colleagues, and indeed all their colleagues' interests, driving wages down and encouraging a general deterioration in employment conditions. They also act against their own self-interest as they cast aside the protection of employment law. Self-employed workers have few rights against unfair dismissal and redundancy, and because holidays, notice periods, sick and maternity pay, and redundancy benefits are criteria used by the Inland Revenue when determining taxation status, such benefits are rarely extended to the self-employed. The resultant savings are again effectively passed to clients – to the general disadvantage of all 'employed' architects as standards of employment (as well as wages) are progressively driven downwards.

It may well suit the mindset of romantic bohemians, whose interests are short-term rather than career-based, and it certainly suits the competitive, though irresponsible, attitudes of our more ruthless employers. Nevertheless, the combined willingness of large numbers of architects – both employers and staff – to breach taxation laws is a process which acts against the interests of the profession and is indeed operating at a level that is shameful.

Both the RIBA and ARB are concerned about this issue and it is to be hoped that disciplinary codes will be further tightened to ensure proper conduct amongst members, both employers and employed. It is also essential that client bodies, particularly state organisations and charities, are persuaded to move away from the current overly harsh tendering procedures which discriminate against legitimate and decent employment conditions. They should demand, as a tendering qualification, some appropriate form of assurance with respect to compliance with taxation requirements – the French do.

Model conditions of employment

Graduates entering law or accountancy receive salaries of £16,500 to £21,000 for three years – their 'training' period – and thereafter annual pay of up to £30,000 within a well structured career offering good benefits and the security of PAYE employment conditions. Not bad for a 24-year-old!

These 'London weighted' figures mark a stark contrast with the prospects in architecture. While accountancy and law trainees often lack a relevant degree, graduates in architecture come with a substantial and directly relevant vocational education and training. Despite this, their conditions of employment are generally poor.

One of the reasons for this is the general deterioration in appointment terms accepted by architects over the last 30 years. It is of course difficult within the volatile construction industry to sustain respectable terms of engagement, but the profession has allowed itself to be ravaged by the demands of lowly and non-paid work. The current lottery bonanza and the extensive use of badly organised and under-rewarded competitions are merely a continuation of the underselling of architects' services.

Bosses carry a heavy responsibility in this respect. At best their supply of cheap architectural labour to an uncaring market is naive. At worst it is immoral pimping on the ill-rewarded efforts of their 'staff' (little better than asking budding actresses to use the casting couch). Make no mistake about it, as long as offices give their services freely – and in this respect an enormous amount of work is simply wasted on a speculative and competitive basis – the conditions for employees in architecture will suffer. It is they who ultimately pay.

Many leading accountants have developed specialist support services to help small and medium-sized firms to handle human resources issues effectively; some offer a review service to identify employment 'irregularities' and highlight opportunities for improving productivity, motivation, commitment and skills. Does your firm need one? Jon Young, head of human resources at Saffery Champness, notes that highly motivated staff are beneficial – whatever the size of a company. Good human resource policies are essential to achieve this, but small firms often miss simple devices and strategies which would enhance motivation and productivity.

Architects as employers are usually dismissive of such advice, yet they continue to preside, all too often, over lousy conditions of employment. Yet there is no reason for a graduate in architecture to expect any less than the terms available within law or accountancy: a proper contract of employment, PAYE salary conditions, respectable levels of pay, and decent conditions with respect to job security, notice, redundancy, sickness, maternity, holidays and ongoing professional development. Enlightened firms might even move towards flexible benefit packages and structured staff training programmes.

We may not like to admit it, but there is extensive exploitation of staff within our profession – and an all-too-strong reminder of the Victorian factory owner about too many of our bosses. This is partly sustained by the view, held by a large proportion of both bosses and workers, that the essential pleasure involved in the 'making' of architecture somehow justifies miserable salaries and disgraceful conditions of employment. This attitude is particularly prevalent amongst 'star' practices. A change of culture is needed.

Peace of mind with PI cover

With the ARB requirement for professional indemnity insurance now mandatory, many architects, especially small practices (and perhaps people 'moonlighting' in parallel with their regular employment), will be arranging PI cover for the first time.

What many professionals forget, when deciding appropriate levels of insurance cover, is to allow for the legal costs that have to be met in the event of any claim. While the ARB has stipulated minimum levels of insurance, this relates to client protection – not yours. So look at your policy wording carefully: some insurers provide cover that includes your legal fees within the limit set, but more usually insurers meet legal costs in addition to the stated indemnity level. If your cover isn't set high enough to meet all the legal costs incurred above and beyond the claim, you may remain exposed – even when your cover exceeds the level of that claim.

Here is a cautionary tale that indicates the importance of setting PI cover appropriately for your own protection.

A small practice, which carried £500,000 cover for each and every claim (including legal costs), felt it was adequately protected: the jobs were of modest size and it had never had a claim in more than 20 years of practice.

Sadly, the apparent mistake of a separately appointed structural engineer necessitated underpinning of a new building in a provincial shopping street. The architect was co-joined in the proceedings and the full extent of his exposure was realised when it was revealed that the engineer had no PI cover and few assets. A nightmare had begun.

The building work cost £136,642, to which was added VAT (which is not recoverable on repairs and thus forms part of the claim), giving a gross construction figure of £160,554. The professional fees for the contract supervision amounted to £25,962 (£30,505 with VAT). Then there was the consequential loss for disruption to the business during a nine-week construction period – a further £38,417. The total claim was valued at £229,476.

The practice had plenty of protection, you might surmise, under the £500,000 cover. Well, you are wrong – it was very tight and cover was all but exhausted. The matter was hard-fought by insurers who maintained that the architect had no liability whatsoever. Total costs for an eight-day trial broke down as follows: the plaintiff's legal fees (including experts in the disciplines of architecture, quantity surveying, geotechnic engineering and structures, together with solicitor and barrister) totalled £118,470 (£139,292 with VAT). With the architect's defence costing £92,340 including VAT, the grand total, including the claim, was £461,018.

Yes, there was just about enough cover, and anyway the defence was successful. But it was a close-run thing – and the architect was well pleased that he had, only that year, raised his PI from £250,000, thus gaining at least some peace of mind during an otherwise traumatic dispute.

Remember, if a dispute runs all the way through court, the actual claim may represent as little as 40 per cent of the total costs you face. If you lose, there are professional fees and VAT on repairs, consequential losses, plus legal and expert fees for both sides, all of which can add up to a killer blow. The only good news is that you can offset VAT on your own side's professional fees.

So be careful when setting your level of PI cover, and ensure that you make adequate provision for legal costs.

Keep your PI details secret

Obviously concerned that I had refused to forward details of my PI Insurer, renewal date, limit of cover, and level of excess in response to the ARB's recent survey, the acting registrar has sent me a letter from which, due to its relevance to our profession, I quote:

'. . . I note your comments concerning confidentiality in respect of professional indemnity insurance but would confirm that your underwriters would allow this to be disclosed to your regulator . . . insurers appreciate that such matters have to be disclosed. Their concern would be disclosure to clients unnecessarily . . .'

This letter raises a fundamental point of great importance to all PI policy holders, because by stating that 'underwriters would allow this to be disclosed' the Acting Registrar is seriously mistaken: I had already discussed this matter with my Insurers and they had expressly instructed me not to give such details to the ARB. Furthermore, they were seriously concerned that such advice had been given by the board.

Insurance companies are understandably wary about revealing PI details to clients or, more to the point, clients' solicitors, and they will draw precious little comfort from the acting registrar's implied willingness to disclose such information to clients in circumstances of alleged necessity. Who at ARB could reliably decide what criteria constitute necessity? And anyway, why should we assume that the ARB can be trusted not to release our PI information whenever requested? It has already shown itself to be alarmingly indiscreet while investigating allegations of negligence against architects.

The point about PI is very simple. Architects carry heavy professional responsibilities and, in our increasingly litigious society, solicitors acting for potential plaintiffs show little restraint in exploiting our professional accountability. They are all too often trigger-happy in their desire to make fat fees by encouraging quite unwarranted claim actions.

Solicitors know that litigation is now so expensive that some insurance companies can be pushed towards out-of-court settlements simply to defray mounting legal costs, even when the architect's performance was sound. Provide such legal teams with the kind of PI details that the ARB is now requesting and you furnish claimants with valuable information which informs their strategy in any claim against you.

Also, if you are co-cited in matters pertaining to other consultants, or to main contractors, sub-contractors or suppliers, your PI information is again invaluable, and may cause litigants to redirect claims principally towards you – especially where others are uninsured, underinsured or have ceased to trade. That is why your Insurer requires the details of your cover to remain strictly confidential throughout any dispute.

Make no mistake – your PI company has contracted with you. Not your client and certainly not the ARB. You have obligations to them under that contract which include allowing them to manage the defence of any claim against you. If you breech the terms of your policy, cover may be withdrawn which is hardly in the interest of your client.

The ARB Code, albeit much discredited and under continuing threat of replacement, requires under Standard 7 that an architect 'should not undertake professional work without adequate and appropriate professional indemnity insurance cover'. Don't misunderstand the word 'should'. Despite the statement in the Code's preamble that it has 'not been drafted in legal language', the previous Registrar assured me that 'should' in this context carries its full legal interpretation – which is 'must'.

So make sure you have PI – you should have done that anyway. If requested, confirm to the ARB that you have complied with Standard 7, but keep all details of your insurer's identity, extent of cover etc totally confidential. And think about it: if the ARB doesn't intend to release details of your PI cover to your clients, then logically they don't need them anyway!

Conversely, if the ARB, as the Registrar's letter clearly implies, is willing to pass on such information in circumstances where it deems such action warranted, you have everything to lose, and your PI company may well hold you responsible for any adverse consequences. You have been warned . . .

Values that inform our work

Taking as his text the Parable of the Talents (Mathew, Chapter 25, verses 14-30) Malcolm Porter, an architect and lay-preacher, recently argued that Christians have a duty to use their skills appropriately. He proffered a challenging question which we, as a profession, might usefully ponder as we celebrate the final Christmas of the twentieth century: are we using our expertise in the best interests of our clients and the community?

Certainly those architects who have endeavoured to undertake socially progressive work have found the 1980s and 90s to be difficult times. This period has seen the consistent erosion of the welfarist programme and the steady dismantling of the state services through which so much of that agenda was delivered – be it housing, schools, hospitals or community centres.

We all know that increased standards of living have led to greater independence and higher expectations; that the cult of the individual has developed at the cost of co-operative endeavours; and that despite the considerable achievements of the health service, the housing programmes, and the education system, the enormous bureaucracies needed to deliver such services were found to be increasingly wanting and cumbersome.

Private sector management and procurement of everything from energy to rail, and from prisons to water supply, was seen as the answer by the crusading Thatcherites. The efforts of successive generations of social reformers, culminating in the heroic achievements of the Atlee government, were discredited and dismissed with a contempt matched only by arrogance.

Then in 1985 came 'Faith in the City', a report that fundamentally challenged the ideology and authority of a Conservative government which had come under increasing critical scrutiny of the established church and a concerned monarchy. Dealing with such difficult and controversial issues as poverty and employment in the inner city, and of council house sales and privatisation, Archbishop Runcie's intervention was as scholarly as it was courageous.

But while a combination of public and institutional concern may have served to temper and even redress the excesses of a government strident (though many would say mistaken) in its commitment to change, we are left at the close of the century with a very different context for working than the one in which most of us trained.

The interests of the consumer are today paramount, and belief in free markets and open competition are deeply incorporated in the culture of our entire procurement system, from 'affordable' housing to university facilities, and from public buildings to health clinics. We have seen the poorly organised and wasteful growth of architectural competitions as a common method of selection; of design-and-build; of 'one-stop shop' appointments and the inevitable sub-contracting of professional services it involves; and of the harsh fee-cutting that is the damaging result of these trends.

In consequence, we witness the ongoing decline in conditions for our so-called 'salaried' architects and smaller firms. Too many in our profession lack decent wages, fair (if any) employment terms, or reasonable job security. Indeed today's 'contract' arrangements for architectural staff amount to little more than the 'lump-labour' arrangements of the 1970s which put a number of construction directors behind bars.

So, as we break for Christmas, I suggest that we reflect carefully on our relationship with those for whom we work. Are we being used properly? Are we able to deliver our services effectively? Are our efforts being squandered?

Sadly, for many, the inevitable conclusion must be that too many of our clients, and too many of our employers, are misusing, abusing and wasting the energy and skills of our profession. Too much time is currently being expended on projects which go nowhere, and too many projects are procured in ways that inevitably lead to failure, dispute and ultimately, litigation.

One immediate challenge in the new century is to secure conditions which enable more within our profession to work with greater efficiency and effect in the delivery of the service that they have, after all, trained so hard to provide.

Happy Christmas.

PART 4

Understanding Legislation

There is no such thing as a waiver

I was grateful to Dr Eric Marchant of Edinburgh University, whose letter (AJ: 20/2/97) was amongst several responses to my recent article on Building Regulation dispensations.

Responding to my suggestion that architects should not place undue reliance on relaxations or dispensations, Dr Marchant suggests that 'the successful development and construction of innovative or non-complying buildings' relies on a system that provides 'waivers, determination, dispensations and relaxations'.

Herein Dr Marchant reveals some of the confusion surrounding this matter: there is no longer any provision for 'waivers' under the current Building Regulations which control building work in England and Wales. Let me explain further: when the Building Regulations 1985 came into force under the 1984 Act, they comprised the Manual to the Building Regulations – a 65-page booklet that set out the regulations and provided explanatory notes – and a series of 'Approved Documents' (listed A to N) which provided 'deemed to satisfy' arrangements for each part of the regulations.

While the manual to the Building Regulations has now of course been withdrawn, the Approved Documents in their revised form are still current. Under Part III of the current Building Regulations 1991, the local authority exercises the Secretary of State's power to dispense with or relax any requirement contained under the Regulations. 'Relaxation' is the process whereby a local authority accepts that because of special circumstances, all the terms of a requirement need not be fully met. 'Dispensation' is agreement by the local authority that 'you need not comply with a requirement at all', which leaves a high level of responsibility with building inspectors (or approved inspectors) when assessing any schemes which fall outside the parameters of Approved Document B.

The requirements of the Building Regulations (1991) are clear and simple with respect to fire. For example, under B1 (Means of Escape), they state only that 'the building shall be designed and constructed so that there are means of escape in case of fire from the building to a place of safety outside the building capable of being safely and effectively used at all material times'. (Requirement B1 does not, incidentally, apply to prisons!)

Thereafter, it is for the applicant to propose a satisfactory arrangement which he should then submit to the local authority (if he elects that they should 'be responsible for supervising the work') in the form of a deposit of 'full plans' or a 'building notice'. Alternatively, if he prefers, the applicant may employ a private 'approved inspector' in which case it is only necessary to give the local authority an 'initial notice' in accordance with the Building (Approved Inspectors etc) Regulations 1985.

There is clearly already adequate scope for innovative and progressive design for those who can justify an alternative approach to Approved Document B. With respect to 'means of escape', relaxations and dispensations are probably inappropriate – the important point is to apply safe fire engineering principles at the early design stage and to subsequently justify those principles under the procedures laid down in the Building Regulations. However, architects should never proceed down a path outside the parameters of the Approved Document without their Client's authority due to the implicit risks of delay – and don't apply for waivers: they simply do not exist.

Dangers when outline consents lapse

A recent case with important planning implications has been brought to my attention. It involves a development of 16 new dwellings in a village, for which the landowner received outline permission in March 1993, subject, as normal, to conditions that building work be started within five years or 'within two years of the date of approval of the last of the reserved matters', and that 'the application for approval of the last of the reserved matters shall be made . . . within three years'.

All straightforward stuff. Happy architect. Very happy client. Land value enhanced. Fees paid. End of commission. The architect copied the client in on the conditions – you must always remember to do this – and received no further instructions . . .

Until, that is, just nine weeks before the expiry of the period allowed for the submission of reserved matters, when the client asked the architect to apply for an extension of time for dealing with those matters. (It was too late, by this time, to prepare and submit a detailed scheme design).

The architect obliged, but the planning authority was unwilling to extend the period of the outline consent without satisfying itself that amendments to the site access could be made to meet the requirements of its new highways officer. (We all build our little empires don't we.) After many months, the application was ultimately recommended to committee for refusal, and refusal was duly notified, thus rendering the status of the land as, once again, agricultural with, of course, a substantial drop in value. Unhappy architect. Very unhappy client!

When refusing consent for the 16 houses, the authority in this case had claimed that since the original application had been determined, the district council had approved a new policy (subsequently incorporated into the deposited district plan) to reduce further 'unwarranted' housing development in order 'to ensure that future developments are sustainable'. It elaborated that the policy was now to renew planning permissions only where 'there is clear evidence of need'. In defining 'need' as 'local needs . . . within the mainly rural area', the council further justified its position by referring to government advice in RPG11 which seeks to limit car based commuting – undeniably the target market for the proposed 16 'executive' homes.

Anticipating all this, the architect had, in his supporting letter, quoted the new edition of Heap's 'Outline Planning Law' (every architect's friend) in which a relevant case heard in the Queen's Bench Division had produced the following ruling: the planning authority shall in such cases, under Section 73 of the Planning Act, consider only the conditions subject to which the planning permission was granted: it should not revisit the basic principles of the application (Corby Borough Council v SoS. for the Environment).

In refusing consent, the decision against the 16 houses represents an apparent halting, if not complete reversal, of the general post-war planning policy which has facilitated a substantial decentralisation to rural areas.

The lesson for anyone still holding a similar outline consent is: DON'T DELAY! Submit details and get building – before the barn door shuts.

The Housing Grants, Construction and Regeneration Act and you

Those of you who read my recent article on warranty agreements for professional 'sub-consultancies' will be interested in the way the now much-vaunted (and sometimes ridiculed) Housing Grants, Construction and Regeneration Act impinges on professional appointments.

Part II starts by giving a rather unexpected description of a construction contract. Included in the definition is 'an agreement with a person for . . . arranging for the carrying out of construction operations by others, whether under sub-contract to him or otherwise'. So architects, whether appointed directly by clients (that would include traditional appointments and design-and-build arrangements) or indirectly as sub-consultants to another lead consultant, are appointed – like it or not – subject to the terms of the new Act. In the event of any conflicts, the Act will, of course, take precedence over all RIBA standard forms.

Perversely, construction contracts include an agreement 'to do architectural design or surveying work' or 'to provide advice on building', where these relate to construction contracts. But is feasibility design work, a planning application or a design competition submission to be included? How remote from the 'construction operation' does an activity have to be to escape? At present it is anybody's guess as there has been no test case. Watch those lawyers' waistlines!

The Act makes clear that construction operations include 'alteration, repair, maintenance, extension . . . whether permanent or not'. Indeed, it appears that the legislators intended all normal construction operations to be included, but I can see more rich pickings in determining the effect of S.105(1), which attempts a comprehensive list of construction operations, and S.105(2), which lists those that are not. It seems ludicrous that minor internal decorations are listed as construction operations while erecting the steel structure for a nuclear reprocessing plant is not.

All contracts with residential occupiers are excluded, including designing that one-off house, however large. But there may be uncertainties here as well – my practice is currently refurbishing the Swedish Ambassador's residence with the most magnificent state function rooms. Does the Act apply here?

But without being too picky, what bearing does the Act have on everyday architectural practice? Well, S.108 provides a right to both parties to refer disputes to immediate adjudication. So, if you fall out with your client or the project manager over payment, you can take the issue straight to the third party to decide. Whether or not you will get a just decision – or indeed any decision – is a matter of intense speculation, but if you do by chance succeed, the decision is binding, unless or until the dispute is finally resolved by arbitration or through legal proceedings.

Secondly, in S.109-113, the Act makes provisions for payment, including entitlement to payment in instalments, which on the face of it look helpful. If not paid when due, then there is now a right to suspend performance (but is this professional?), and there is a general prohibition on pay-when-paid provisions.

Believe me, though, the big employers will continue to bully small consultants, for parties 'are free to agree the amounts of the payments and the intervals at which, or the circumstances in which, they become due'. As we all know, being free to agree usually means resigned acceptance of imposed terms.

A CDM nightmare

A disturbing case involving CDM work has recently come to my attention.

An architect had been appointed to oversee repairs and fit-out work to a high street building in a small provincial town. The job value was only £57,000. A wall was being removed so structural work was involved. The architect had thought CDM legislation did not apply because the job was so small, and had not mentioned the CDM Regulations to the client. In the rush to meet the client's programme, a budget had been agreed at an early stage with a small firm of builders which would organise trade and labour as necessary.

Demolition proceeded apace and work was well under way when the CDM issues were brought to the architect's attention. With much embarrassment the architect had to explain to the client that a planning supervisor was required. To make matters worse, the planning supervisor, once appointed, immediately informed the architect that further irregular progressing of the work constituted a criminal act, and set out the basis upon which the situation could be regularised – stop all work, appoint a principal contractor, prepare a Health and Safety plan etc.

The builder, much out of his depth, had never heard of CDM legislation, and upon being asked to accept an appointment as principal contractor – and being of rough and ready character – promptly marched off site, never to return. Cost control was immediately put at risk (could a new builder be found at the same contract price?) and the construction programme and completion date were at once threatened.

The architect was in difficulty because he had been party to the letting of a contract, however informal, without proper provisions as necessary to comply with the CDM Regulations (the client had not been made aware of his duties – neither a planning supervisor nor a principal contractor had been appointed – and at no stage had a health and safety plan been prepared). All very messy, and potentially an issue for the architect's P.I. insurers.

The architect should, of course, have known better: the CDM

legislation had come into force in July 1994 under the Construction (Design and Management) Regulations 1994. While this legislation was prompted by corresponding European directives, there had previously been concern within the construction industry that designers frequently generated hazardous and unsafe site activities through their approach to design, or through the content of their specification. By making designers more responsible for the consequences of their work in terms of safety during construction stages, and by subjecting designers to a formal review at pre-tender stage with respect to the safety aspects of their design and specification work, it was intended that site conditions would be greatly improved and that accident and injury levels would in turn be reduced. That, in brief, is the background and intent of this legislation.

I shall offer some guidance on the basic procedures for compliance with this legislation in the following half dozen articles.

A guide to CDM legislation

I set out below a summary of how the CDM regulations apply to all construction work, and place obligations on the client, all consultants with a design or specification role, the planning supervisor and principal contractor (both of whom may have to be appointed) and all other contractors and sub-contractors.

The regulations enshrine two levels of control. For all projects which move from feasibility stage to a 'commitment to build' there is a requirement for consultants to carry out risk assessments on their design and specification work – among the 'design considerations', they should have regard to minimising or avoiding risks to those constructing and maintaining the building, and also communicate any hazards in their documentation. The second level of control involves the introduction of a planning supervisor and principal contractor – it is only required for those projects that meet certain further criteria.

If the client lives, or will live, in the premises concerned, and the building work is to be carried out directly for him, then the additional provisions do not apply – whatever the scale of the works, and even if they involve demolition. For all those projects other than private residential, the threshold for the additional provisions coming into force is defined as follows: 'If the work is expected to last longer than 30 days . . . or the work is expected to involve more than 500 person days of construction work. . . or more than four people are expected to be carrying out work at any one time'. However, if the project involves demolition or dismantling (whatever the scale) then the additional provisions apply in any event. Probably the clearest (and graphic) guidance on duties under the regulations appears in 'Designing for Health and Safety in construction' (HSE books).

There are some strange inconsistencies in the application of these regulations. For example, a large, complex project involving a constrained site, demolition and a multiplicity of trades need have no planning supervisor or principal contractor if the client is a private individual and the project is a dwelling. Is this because fewer accidents occur in domestic construction work, or because the legislators decided that they should not apply such stringent controls to domestic situations? It would be interesting to know whether any statistics exist to show the proportion of accidents occurring on domestic and non-domestic projects – both before and after the introduction of the regulations – to see whether this inconsistency is justified.

The effect of the very low threshold for the full application of the regulations to non-domestic works is that some experienced and competent small builders are unable, or unwilling, to try to satisfy the planning supervisor that they are competent principal contractors. It is not that they cannot manage the site, the sub-contractors and the works in a competent way – it is that they are unable or unwilling to do it and demonstrate that they are doing it through the medium of paperwork.

It will be bad for the industry if skilled small contractors are forced out of the non-domestic sector where, in the view of many architects, such contractors produce the best work, with the least problems and arguments. Indeed, such an outcome would be seen as yet another indication of this society's desire to trade skilled craftsmen for paper-pushing bureaucrats.

Your duties as a Planning Supervisor

In the last column I outlined the circumstances in which the CDM Regulations apply. Here is some guidance on the main obligations which arise.

At inception, advise the client if he/she has duties under these regulations. These may include:

● The appointment of a planning supervisor.

● The appointment of a principal contractor.

● Ensuring construction work does not begin until a suitable Health and Safety plan has been prepared.

A planning supervisor should be appointed as early as possible within the design process – his job is firstly to ensure that all consultants consider health and safety issues throughout the design stages, and that in this respect their work is co-ordinated. Secondly, he must ensure that sufficient information is made available to contractors regarding the risks with respect to the construction procedures that are inherent within the design. This takes the form of a health and safety plan which the planning supervisor usually produces himself. It supplements the main contract tender documents and provides summary information on particular risks which should in the first instance be described within the design consultant's drawings and specification work. The plan can be brief – its purpose is to communicate essential information to contractors who are ultimately responsible for using safe construction methods – and who should therefore take these methods into account in their planning and pricing of the works.

The planning supervisor's final task in the pre-construction phase is to assist the client in ensuring that the principal contractor further develops the health and safety plan in readiness for the start of work on site.

Contrary to popular opinion, the planning supervisor has no formal role in the construction phase, with the exception of reviewing any further design work which is carried out during the construction period (for example in a management contract or design and build contract situation).

Upon completion of the construction work, it is the planning supervisor's duty to ensure that a health and safety file is prepared and handed over to the client, who should keep it available for use by those who will maintain, repair and alter the building in the future.

While it is now a condition of JCT contracts that the health and safety file be provided by the principal contractor prior to practical completion, it is often, as we all know, difficult to extract information from contractors and subcontractors at the end of a project. Accordingly, insistence on the provision of a draft of the health and safety file well before practical completion and the threat of withholding of monies until the complete file is delivered are both wise precautions. Authority for such actions should therefore be enshrined in the contract documents and routinely enforced by the project architect.

The regulations do not preclude an architect from being planning supervisor for his own project. Indeed it is arguable that the breadth of knowledge of the design disciplines, construction process and contractual matters make the architect the professional best equipped to carry out this role. However, there may be good reason for appointing someone other than the project architect to the supervisor's role – even if he is another architect within the same firm – as this provides better for the independence that is an implicit requirement of the role.

Practical completion and CDM

Be very careful in the heat of a building handover not to contravene the CDM Regulations when issuing your practical completion certificate. You could be in very serious trouble – especially if your firm has also acted as planning supervisor.

Adam Voelcker, in his recent letter (AJ 9.10.97), claims that it is often difficult to obtain the contractor's health and safety file. You know all the routine excuses: unavailable specialist information from sub-contractors etc. Such excuses simple won't do, cannot be accepted, and will not provide any defence for the architect who issues his practical completion certificate without having ensured compliance with CDM Regulations.

Of course, there is enormous pressure on the architect, especially on commercial work. We've all been there: client screaming to move in, developer frantic for your certificate to trigger purchaser's payment, contractor feigning desperation over mounting l&a damages, snagging lists as long as your arm . . . Practical completion is already a legal minefield and now, to add to our worries, there are new and stringent obligations under CDM!

Well, relax, have a coffee, and let's rehearse them together.

First, contractual obligations: new amendments published in 1995 introduce into each JCT contract a clause requiring the contractor to provide 'within the time reasonably required' the necessary information for the health and safety file which the planning supervisor compiles and issues to the client at practical completion stage.

This obligation is underpinned by an amendment to the previous practical completion clause, which states that the contractor must comply 'sufficiently with clause 6A.4' as a pre-condition to the issue of a practical completion certificate under clause 17.1 (see Amendment 14 to JCT 80, issued March 1995).

So, even if the building is otherwise practically complete, the certificate must not be issued until the contractor has complied with his duties in relation to the Health & Safety file. During this time, l&a damages may be levied, retention monies withheld, and the commencement of the defects liability period postponed. Measures against the contractor for non-compliance are accordingly draconian.

Second, let's look at statutory obligations: the health and safety file contains information to enable the building and its systems to be understood, operated, maintained and altered safely. This information typically includes details of construction and materials that may present hazards; 'as built' drawings of services; operating and maintenance instructions for all equipment and systems; and manufacturers' technical literature. Such information could be crucial to the safe use of, say, a window-cleaning cradle suspension system, and an 'interiors' company may rely on the Health and Safety file when fitting-out a new development. If, following an accident, this information is found to be missing, or incomplete, criminal charges could be brought against the planning supervisor if he has failed in his duties. He should accordingly warn against the issue of a practical completion certificate until his work is complete.

Heaven help the office that, having acted as architect and planning supervisor, issues a practical completion certificate in breach of the CDM Regulations.

Mr Voelcker has raised an important issue: of ten practices I asked, only one small office in Hereford (run by my father, Derek Hyett) is applying revision 6A.4 of JCT Clause 17.1 correctly. They are, of course, clever people down there in the Marches.

An introduction to adjudication

The old adage goes: 'Professions are there to get you out of trouble, but architects put you in it.' There can be no doubt (because we preside over the conversion of large sums of money into assets that are fixed) there is some truth in it. We increase our clients' wealth but we devastate their cash balances. Trouble comes when our employers have made wrong predictions and allowances, for then not only are they in trouble, but so are we. We may not even get paid.

In the past we have relied on 'Order 14' summary judgement – or the threat of it. But the catch with summary judgement is that the applicant must show that there is no possible defence to the claim. This has always been a conspicuous hindrance, for it is surprisingly easy for clients to convince a judge that alleged shortfalls in an architect's services should at least be investigated through the processes of litigation, even if allegations are ultimately found to be without any foundation.

So, welcome to the fast-track, rough-justice adjudication procedures under the Housing Grants, Construction and Regeneration Act 1996. Much has already been written about them, but little has been made of the usefulness of adjudication for securing due payment for professional services.

Section 108 of the HGCR Act sets the parameters. A dispute is given the widest definition, for it is to include any difference. But that difference must have arisen under the contract and not, for instance, out of or in connection with it. You can therefore ask an adjudicator to order payment of interest on your late-paid fees only if you have bothered to complete the relevant section in the appointment document; if you left it blank, you will have to rely on arbitration or the courts to reimburse all those bank charges and interest you have grudgingly paid during the long wait.

The overriding advantages of adjudication are that you can start it at any time; and if there is a defence to be made against the claim for payment, then it has to be stated and tested. There is no opportunity for procrastination.

The timetable for adjudication is terrifically fast, and serious doubts must be raised about the practicality of dealing with complex issues of construction claims in such a short space of time. But for the simple objective of being paid fees, the period of seven days for the appointment of the adjudicator and then 28 for a decision should be plenty.

Unless the parties agree, the decision of an adjudicator is not final in determining a dispute. It has force because it is binding on the parties until the dispute is finally determined by legal proceedings, by arbitration (if the contract provides for it) or by agreement. This should therefore be a welcome end to the ploy of using litigation and arbitration simply as devices for deferring payment.

Late payment of fees was one of the foremost reasons for introducing this piece of legislation, so let's make it work. It will be no good at all unless we are prepared to use it, and use it so readily and swiftly that adjudication becomes an expectation – and thus an effective deterrent. It could transform bad payers' habits.

An adjudication crisis

Imagine you are the job architect with a £36 million new building under construction, and on site there is a hut full of the contractor's surveyors dedicated to cooking up claims!

The first test pile fails dramatically following the clerk of work's reports of excessive delays to concrete pouring. Then, after some stiff meetings between the contractor's and employer's engineers, you are advised that the landfill conditions warrant an increase to pile depths. The site agent (doubtless prompted by his surveyors) tells you that these new circumstances necessitate a bigger piling rig which cannot be obtained for three weeks. Under clause 25 he notifies delay, citing not only variation (even though the pile design is a contractor responsibility), but also knock-on effects including encroaching winter weather and the Christmas holiday.

Confounding all logic, consecutive measurements of the next pile tested go from pass to fail – to pass again. 'Better safe than sorry,' says the engineer as she forthrightly condemns the second test. Meanwhile, you refuse an extension of time, stating that the first pile failure was caused by the delayed concrete pouring and known landfill conditions. (Get your friendly engineer to explain the technicalities if you don't understand.)

The contractor objects to both decisions. Alarmed, you report to your angered employer saying that you cannot accept the responsibility of countermanding the engineer. You forewarn him to expect an adjudication notice, which promptly arrives next morning by registered post. Two issues are referred: to open up the architect's failure to give an extension of time, and to declare that the second test pile is good. A second letter brings another clause 25 notice, citing the adjudication itself as force majeure and the adjudicator as a statutory undertaker. It seeks agreement for the adjudicator to decide these matters on the grounds that the contractor had lost faith in the architect's ability to reach any objective decision in the matter.

The appointed adjudicator is a quantity surveyor so the contractor sends him an especially thick wad of engineering technicalities that he cannot possibly comprehend, insisting the adjudication be completed within the 28 days allowed by the Act. Chaos ensues! The decision on the second pile is reversed (who legally carries responsibility? The adjudicator doesn't) and an 11-week extension is granted; too long even when allowing time for the adjudication stoppage. Overall a bad result – but non-negotiable. Because of the adjudication procedures, the engineers fall further behind, causing yet more delays . . .

Back to reality: three weeks ago my partner Ian Salisbury conducted the first ever adjudication applying the procedures of the HGCR Act (see AJ 11.6.98). The dispute was over fee payment and all parties agreed the process had been successful. But the issues were relatively simple. When a dispute involves complicated issues, adjudication is far less likely to reach a satisfactory conclusion, and the tale above illustrates the kind of dreadful tangles that will emerge when complex disputes are subjected to the new adjudication procedures.

Such tangles will inevitably lead to calls for a major review of the Act. Meanwhile, architects have a duty to anticipate contractors' referrals to adjudication, and maintain a level of preparedness that will protect their employers' positions. This will carry attendant costs – so allow for them in your fees!

The heavy cost of adjudication

If you don't know who carried the can for the adjudicator's wrong decision on the pile test I asked you to imagine last week, don't worry; we are now many months further on, and that particular case is going to the House of Lords.

This week I want to give further consideration to the less exotic part of my example: extensions of time. This will be fertile soil for the nightmare adjudication that may soon be heading your way.

You are on the same job – a £6 million contract to run over 90 weeks. Early on, you remember, the adjudicator declared the dodgy pile test satisfactory and granted an additional 11-week extension of time, beyond the seven weeks already granted by you as architect.

You refused several further notices of delay during the ensuing months, showing from progress records, labour returns, and the record of monthly valuations, that the contractor was simply failing to manage his resources properly. To your great relief there were no further adjudications and eventually practical completion was signed, albeit with a 35-week overrun beyond the 18 weeks already confirmed through the earlier adjudication.

Your review of extensions of time added nothing more and the furious contractor informed you that if 35 weeks were not granted, then they would 'most certainly' be secured by adjudication! Within the hour comes the adjudication notice citing almost every architect's instruction and every drawing issue as a cause of delay and disruption, with every notice to be opened up and reviewed, and claiming an incredible £4.6 million in addition to the original contract sum.

Another adjudicator is appointed and, seven days after the notice, five immensely heavy volumes arrive, the proud product of the industrious site surveyors.

Now, although this is between builder and employer, make no mistake: it's about to become a serious problem for you. The surveyors took months preparing the claim and there are only seven days in which to reply, and believe me, without a well-prepared employer's defence, the contractor may well get away with it.

And an additional worry emerges: your employer has been advised to adjudicate against you to hedge the likely result of the building adjudication. The same adjudicator is appointed, and now you know with near certainty that the contractor's carefully prepared claim (no matter how shamefully inflated) will likely stick in part, and that part on you. For your employer has carefully deployed the argument that 'if anything has gone wrong it surely cannot be my fault'.

This is deeply worrying for your insurer and puts your excess at great risk. Another bad decision will, of course, be put right in a year's time by arbitration, but don't think it's all over. Four months later, when it is time to renew your PI policy, your broker telephones to advise that your insurer (aware of the adjudication outcome) is declining to renew your policy. The only option you have to stay in practice (remember those ARB regulations?) is to pay a hugely inflated premium to another PI company.

Meanwhile, cracks begin to open in the blockwork due to the faulty pile, condemned by you on the engineer's advice, but subsequently 'authorised' by the adjudicator. Responsibility for the losses arising out of that mistake will be a key test case.

Airships, racing cars and the professional risks of working in Europe

As the 1997 Formula One season gets properly under way, the sad events that have overtaken Frank Williams following the death of Ayrton Senna cast a long shadow over motor-racing . Of course Senna's death was tragic, despite its occurrence in a sport where risk and brinkmanship are the essential ingredients of delight and entertainment , but it is difficult for us in England to understand how Williams and his two partners (together with the three racing officials from the San Marino circuit) can find themselves charged with 'culpable homicide' as a result of the crash .This is without precedent in a sport which has, throughout its history, claimed the lives of many drivers.

If found guilty in a trial which is expected to last six months, Frank Williams could be jailed (author's note: he wasn't), although a fine or a suspended prison sentence is more probable. The general belief is, however, that all the defendants will be acquitted, so why do the Italians have a penchant for these extraordinary trials ?

They effected a similar response in 1928 after disaster had struck the Italian adventurer Umberto Nobile during his second mission of discovery over the North Pole in his airship 'Italia', the sequel to his much acclaimed voyage in 'Norge' in 1925. A combination of freezing fog and gales caused the airship to nose dive and crash, spilling Nobile, his dog, eight survivors and much equipment out onto the ice. Relieved of so much weight, Italia lurched back into the air with six doomed and frightened crewmen on board and vanished through the clouds, never to be seen again.

Like motor-racing (indeed even more so), airship design and development involved great risks and placed enormous demands on the design teams struggling at the cutting edge of technology. Yet despite having brought past glory to Italy, Nobile, who with his dog Titina was eventually rescued, returned home to face accusations of negligence and incompetence. As a result Italian airship development was permanently ended. Surely such a fate could not overtake the beloved Ferrari.

The Italian authority's response to such events of course has very serious implications for other professionals working in Italy in any circumstances where death or injury may arise as a result of alleged design or construction failure. Accordingly, UK architects active in Italy should take heed: we do not expect to end up in the slammer as a result of routine design error here, but, as the Senna crash shows, this is a very distinct possibility in Italy.

As there is now a mandatory requirement to tender all member-state projects throughout the European Community, the conditions under which those projects are carried out, at least with respect to the interpretation of criminal culpability, should surely be consistently applied. However, the Williams experience clearly demonstrates that Italian architects involved in building failures over here face fairer treatment with respect to negligence claims   than our architects can expect in Italy: criminal charges might be raised there which would be unthinkable under UK law.

Unfortunately, in Europe (at least with respect to the Italians) the playing field is distinctly uneven as far as professional risk pertaining to design and supervision work is concerned. This is very unsatisfactory and needs review.

PART 5

Handling disputes

What to do if you get a subpoena

So what should you do if a subpoena arrives in your morning post? The answer is: nothing. It's invalid so just ignore it. Strict regulations require that a subpoena must be served personally on the individual named on it – not by post.

A subpoena is a writ ordering a person to attend a law court as a witness. It carries the authority of the State and takes precedence over all your other work and holidays. No compensation is payable for any consequential losses arising through the issue of a writ: there is no responsibility on a solicitor to pay those subpoenaed a fee for anything other than disbursements.

Threatened with a subpoena during a contractor/sub-contractor dispute, I once agreed to co-operate to avoid its issue on condition that the acting solicitor paid my time and costs, and that a record of the discussion together with a copy of all 'revealed' documents was subsequently passed to the other side. Because I could see no harm in providing factual information in an effort to assist in the early resolution of the dispute, and by taking the initiative, I was able to manage events to suit my programme and benefit our account. (But always get clearance from your indemnity insurer before making such agreements and avoid giving information that incriminates you.)

Subpoenas come in two forms: duces tecum (appear with documents) and ad testificandum (to testify). Withholding information is not an option: it can lead to fines of up to £10,000 or even imprisonment – the court's powers in this respect are draconian. In one case, a doctor who refused to release medical records material to a court action was subpoenaed and kept waiting for days until he co-operated.

It is important to think carefully before acting. Some subpoenas are issued simply in the hope that a witness holds something useful (ie without good grounds for believing that the witness can in fact provide evidence pertinent to the case). Try to understand your relevance to the dispute, as a justified challenge will often result in such subpoenas being set aside as improper 'fishing expeditions'.

Other areas where subpoenas are frequently defective are: expiry (it must be served properly within 12 weeks of the date of issue); short service (it must be served not less than four days, excluding weekends, before the day on which court attendance is demanded); necessary leave (if the subpoena requires attendance in chambers rather than court, the leave of the court is required prior to issue); oppression (where the true motive of compelling inspection of documents is to see whether the party issuing the subpoena might have a cause of action against the witness and thus may be viewed as an abuse and set aside accordingly). So check it carefully.

Even the print font size (must be not smaller than 11 point type for printing or elite type for typography) and margin sizes (at least 1.5ins must be left blank on the left hand side of the page) can lead to a subpoena being set aside as defective.

Therefore, upon receipt of a subpoena establish its validity: many solicitors just 'try it on'. Where appropriate, notify your indemnity insurer and if necessary take legal advice. Never blindly ignore a subpoena; heavy fines can be imposed on those who disregard one which been properly issued. Suspension of your services due to imprisonment will hardly impress your other clients.

Managing your dispute

You are up to your eyes in a dispute with your client. The most common scenario is that you have reluctantly sued for long-outstanding fees at the conclusion of work. Either the job didn't proceed (client couldn't acquire site/secure loans/secure planning) or despite reaching practical completion the client won't pay your latest account.

Or perhaps there is a genuine reason for grievance. If so, it will almost certainly be due to poor administrative/contractual performance or technical failure. (It's very rare for architects to 'mess up' on basic spatial planning: the stairs rarely arrive in the en-suite bathroom; and subjective design issues are almost unheard of in litigation).

Anyway, the row is on so how should you handle it? Well, don't take it personally (he who never made a mistake never did anything). Disputes, already common, will become even more so as an ever greater proportion of jobs get set up badly (with conditions and objectives that are unachievable) and as lawyers (especially where legal aid will in future be denied) encourage litigation on a 'success-only' fee basis.

So look objectively at the situation - and LEARN, both for now and for the future. By understanding your position, you can begin to structure your dispute resolution strategy and/or help those who will be guiding you, and you may avoid such pitfalls again.

Next, and pretty sharp, inform your PI insurer. If in doubt DO IT ANYWAY! Late notification may void your policy, and generally they are nice people who are there to help.

If you are commencing the action, be careful on two counts. First, you are still under an obligation to notify your insurer if a counterclaim for unpaid fees materialises. Second, and with that in mind, choose your solicitor carefully at the outset. Insurers usually insist on appointing one of their preferred firms to defend, and, as the claim and counterclaim are normally best handled by one lawyer, your solicitor may not be retained and you will face abortive fees. Best to find someone acceptable to insurers from the start.

Where you know the fault is yours, and the issue is relatively small (but be careful here because disputes usually escalate, and there may be consequential costs), you might consider settling the matter yourself. As one builder once said to me, there is no problem that can't be solved, it's just a matter of who pays! This may be highly controversial advice which breaches all rules, but we did just this – once – and were well pleased with the result.

Essentially, ambiguity on our drawings had led to 'creaky' floors (the boards should have been screwed not nailed) on a £400,000 project. Good, long-standing client. Good builder. Unhappy mess. Whose fault? Definitely not the client's! Remedy: furniture out, carpets up, and lots of labour over three weekends. The builder and I agreed to split a cost-only account. I wrote the cheque, albeit with some pain, a week later.

Result? Five years on we have done a further three buildings, worth some £270,000 in fees, for the same client. He liked our conciliatory approach. Should I have notified our Insurers? Well, we faced a problem not a dispute, and we solved it – so arguably not.

Should ARB be notified? Not on your life!

Wobbly bridges and straight apologies

If Lord Foster looks carefully through binoculars from his Thameside offices, he will see a long redundant sign instructing soldiers marching towards Chelsea Barracks to 'break step', just as Roman centurions did when crossing bridges, in order to mitigate the effect of marching in unison. It is therefore all the more surprising that this problem was not properly anticipated in the design of the Millennium Bridge linking St Paul's with the Tate Modern.

But it wasn't and, regrettably,it will surely be forever dubbed 'the wobbly bridge' – even after repair work has been carried out. To Foster's eternal humiliation, the project has become a yardstick for measure: crossing a perilously unstable rope bridge over a ravine near Lands End recently, I heard someone ask 'does this wobble more than the one in London'.

A Millennium Bridge Trust spokesperson has said that no one knows how money for repairs is going to be raised, although shadow culture secretary Peter Ainsworth, when branding the project 'a national embarrassment', suggested that a private sector solution should be found. Very imaginative, and about as easy as selling fridges to Eskimos.

But even if no one yet knows how to repair it, the liability and responsibility for funding remedial work is pretty clear. Despite the criticism that he has attracted by insisting that the failure is an engineering rather than an architectural issue, Foster is of course correct. I have no axe to grind on this one, being a huge admirer of Arups, but it seems most likely that, barring any third party responsibility, it is the engineer's insurers who will ultimately pick up the tab.

Unless, that is, Foster had been told that the design concept would inevitably be subject to excessive movement against the otherwise welcome rhythm of marching art lovers and tourists. But the bottom line is that it was an implicit, if not explicit, requirement that the 'bridge too tight' should be tolerably stable in use. The duty to meet that objective lay principally with Arups, and the continued refusal to allow public access is clear evidence that the current levels of movement are outside acceptable limits.

Against such circumstances, remedial work is as essential as litigation is (alas, probably) inevitable.

Damages will of course include fat earnings for lawyers and, if design responsibility is ultimately transferred to other engineers, professional fees will also be claimed against their work. The client has a duty, however, to mitigate losses so he will not rush to replace Arups even if patience is wearing a bit thin, and in any event who better than the best to sort this mess out?

Against any eventual claim, the defence can set off the costs of betterment – that is any work that would have been required in the first instance to make the 'bridge of plight' safe, albeit only at the cost that would have been incurred within the original contract. It seems unlikely that any losses accrue from the ongoing closure: not being a toll bridge there is no shortfall in revenue. That said, there may be a claim for lost interest against capital 'tied up' in a non-functioning facility, but that would be difficult to pursue.

So, despite living in the age of apology (even Tony Blair now believes it apprpriate to say 'sorry' for his part in the Dome saga), it is wholly inappropriate to expect Foster to assume any responsibility for the 'blade not right'. He expected that the basic engineering solution would be effective and is surely as dismayed as the rest of us that it isn't.

And it is important for us all, as architects, that he stands firm where others would surely wobble, for the division of responsibility between consultants must, as far as possible, be maintained. Our work is risky enough without being expected to assume blame for the faults of others. That said, it seems that even one as experienced in public relations as Lord Foster could learn how to pass the buck a little more gracefully.

Architects' Journal 5.10.00

Weaknesses in education affect your PI premiums

Few people realise the close inter-relationship between those responsible for drafting the RIBA's various standard forms of agreement documents (SFAs), the courts, and the professional indemnity insurance companies.

Let me explain. When an architect is brought before a court of law to face allegations of negligence or incompetence (and few people including those in charge of discipline at the ARB distinguish between these charges), two questions will inevitably go to the heart of the issues.

First, what did the architect do that he/she shouldn't have done? For example, issue a practical completion certificate without having inspected the work. Second, what didn't he do that he should have done? For example, failed to comply with listed buildings legislation.

Likewise, when complaints relating to competence are referred to the ARB, often at the conclusion of the processes of litigation in the civil courts, similar questions will be addressed when determining the appropriate action to take against an individual architect.

What is the benchmark against which performance is measured? Certainly case law can assist the courts (although apparently not the ARB because its last Registrar destroyed all past 'case' files dating from the old registration council!) Then there is the opinion of the expert witness who can advise the court with respect to what a reasonably competent architect should have (or should not have) done in such circumstances. Reference can, of course, be made to the RIBA Job Book (now up to its 7th edition), but the weaknesses here are twofold: first this publication does not form part of the contract between architect and client, and second it is no longer compatible with the latest SFAs.

So the main point of reference in assessing an architect's performance is the letter or SFA under which the appointment is made. Here, the courts and the ARB can establish the scope of the service commissioned (ie full/partial basic services, 'other' services etc.). Furthermore, the duties under each work stage are clearly set out in the SFAs (albeit that I remain critical of these documents for a range of reasons including those outlined previously in AJ 20.4.2000 & 27.4.2000).

So it becomes quickly apparent that the extent of the PI insurer's liabilities are principally determined by the RIBA's SFA publications which define the scope of services to be provided. Likewise, the ARB relies on these documents in determining what could reasonably have been expected of any architect against whom a complaint is made.

But if architects are unable to provide services in accordance with the obligations that can be expected under the SFAs, then the PI companies are of course exposed to risk. This introduces a further and crucial element into the equation: are the schools of architecture preparing graduates properly, in terms of both the scope and the quality of service that will be defined as appropriate by the courts against the duties set out in the various SFAs?

The schools may not welcome such scrutiny, but this is an important issue: those graduates from Part 2 courses who decide to press on and sit professional practice exams quite reasonably expect that their education will have prepared them appropriately: where they have studied conscientiously. They anticipate early success in their Part 3 exams, and they look forward to being able to perform competently in practice.

But when things go wrong and architects are sued successfully, it's pay-out day for the insurers. And in consequence, of course, PI premiums go up for the rest of us.

This is just another reason why it is in the interest of our profession that the education provided for those who wish to enter practice as architects – by far the majority of students – will prepare them properly with respect to the professional obligations that they will have to meet. Apart from serving the consumer competently, and maintaining the reputation of our profession, it is crucial that the levels of successful PI claims is kept to the minimum – otherwise we all pay dearly through constantly escalating premiums.

A roof departs, a new claim starts

I learned recently of an elaborate high-tech roof canopy arrangement in the north of England which collapsed with near disastrous results during strong winds.

The canopy had formed a projecting part of a large mono-pitch roof to a headquarters building. It was supported by a series of raking struts which should have been connected by clockwise and anti-clockwise threads at opposing ends into pre-formed 'threaded' sockets in the fascia beam and vertical mullions.

Unfortunately, while both the architect and structural engineer were consistent in showing this arrangement in their drawings, the steelwork supplier, who was also responsible under a 'domestic' sub-contract arrangement for the frame assembly and erection, had departed from the intended design. This was despite the incorporation of the correct arrangement within his own 'shop fabrication drawings' which had routinely been issued to the main contractor following consultant comments. As later become evident, the struts had been manufactured with the required thread at the top, but not the bottom. Following construction, and for the entire life of the occupied building up until the storm, the struts had therefore merely 'rested' within the sockets incorporated into the vertical mullion structure.

The gale force wind which ultimately wreaked such havoc lifted the overhanging roof sufficiently to cause the struts to pull clear of the mullion 'sockets', at which point, and under their enormous load, the fascia beam collapsed. The roof sheeting which overhung the entrance area buckled upwards and the wind then lifted the metal sheeting, ripping some 40 per cent of the roof covering away, causing much damage in the process. One sheet hit a car being driven along a nearby road although, very fortunately, it caused no injury to the driver.

During the subsequent litigation, the sub-contractor claimed to have issued the structural engineer with a formal request to change the lower cruciform fixing from threaded to welded connection. However, no record of such a request existed and neither the architect, engineer, builder or building inspector had had any reason to expect any other arrangement would be built than that which was originally intended and consistently illustrated on all contract drawings. When assembled and painted, there was no evidence to suggest that the strut/mullion connection was any other than the properly prescribed threaded fixing. Clearly, the sub-contractor had been irresponsible and grossly negligent in departing from the drawings without approval.

With considerable decency and goodwill, the main contractor put the building right at his own cost and then successfully pursued the sub-contractor for damages.

However, technical experts who were subsequently engaged to investigate the failure on behalf of the steelwork sub-contractor discovered that the roofing sub-contractors had themselves departed from the specified roofing system by using a screw to fix the metal sheeting that was a different size to that prescribed in the manufacturer's literature. Accordingly, the steelwork sub-contractor mounted a spirited defence against the full extent of damages, arguing that the loss of roof sheeting would not have occurred had the correct screws been used.

The poor architect, who had until then appeared innocent, moved centre stage under allegations of poor supervision and found himself facing a serious claim. Ultimately the sub-contractor's case, which was never tested in court, collapsed – but not before some considerable costs in defence of this spurious claim had been incurred by the architect.

Had the matter gone to court, the judge would have considered the related responsibility of the architect and engineer. (For further dicussion of the principles raised, see the article beginning on page124.)

Are final certificates final?

A decision last month by His Honourable Judge Humphrey Lloyd has far-reaching implications for architects and the construction industry.

Oxford University Fixed Assets Ltd had engaged the plaintiff, Wimpey Construction Ltd, under the 1980 JCT standard form of contract (private with quantities) to build a combined pharmacology and neuropharmacology centre; at some £9 million, a very nice job indeed.

In the action, the plaintiff alleged that blockwork partitions constructed during 1990 'were abnormally and unacceptably wet . . . so that when they dried out widespread cracking was caused, particularly to the plasterwork which had been applied to the blockwork'. (Who among us hasn't faced this problem?)

Practical completion was certified by Architects Design Partnership (the defendant) in July 1991, and in August 92 Wimpey received lists of defects that included cracked plaster which it duly repaired, though evidently unsuccessfully because the architect issued a further list of 'cracking' defects in November 93. Following yet more remedial work, in early 94 the architects eventually issued a certificate of making good of defects, followed by a final certificate.

Sadly all appears to have been far from well because in July 97 the university issued a writ claiming damages for negligence and breach of the contractual duty of care owed by the architect. The allegations included failure to ensure the 'blockwork was not wet'; failure to ensure faulty work was rectified; negligent issue of the certificates of practical completion and making good defects; negligent issue of the final certificate; failure to investigate the cause of the cracking; and failure to recommend enforcement of the contract. But for the issue of the final certificate, the plaintiff would have held Wimpey liable and the claim really boiled down to loss of that opportunity.

The judge had to decide whether the final certificate provided conclusive evidence that the quality of materials and the standard of workmanship were to the reasonable satisfaction of the architect, and if so, whether the contractor had discharged his duty under contract, and if he had whether the third party claim against Wimpey must fail.

Mr Taverner (for Wimpey) agreed, rather optimistically, that the final certificate provided conclusive evidence that the work was not defective at the time of its issue, saying that the work was either never defective, or, if it had once been defective, the defects had been put right.

The judge assumed that the defects in the blockwork constituted damage which occurred prior to the issue of the final certificate (ie it was not a latent defect) and he went on to conclude that while Wimpey might have carried out remedial works to the satisfaction of the architect, it had not done them in accordance with its obligations under contract.

Nevertheless, the judge decided that 'the effect of the final certificate was not that Wimpey had no liability, but that Wimpey ceased to be liable'. Pointing out that neither party to the contract had challenged the final certificate within the 28-day period allotted for that purpose, the judge concluded that the issue of the certificate by the architect was 'tantamount to a decision discharging the liability of the contractor'.

Third party proceedings against Wimpey were dismissed with costs. This ruling, over what is after all a relatively simple issue, shows just how onerous contract administration can be. Such risks should surely be reflected by reward!

Your right to rely on others

I recently recounted the story of a dispute arising from the structural collapse of a projecting roof canopy. Despite the steel fabricator's negligence, arising through his failure to securely connect structural supports, the unfortunate architect found himself centre stage in terms of alleged responsibility for the consequences, which put the building out of action and the repair costs at over £250,00.

This claim was never tested in court, because the sub-contractor's Insurer settled, but had matters progressed to litigation the judge would have considered (among many issues) whether the architect and/or consultant engineer had any responsibility for the structural failure: they had both provided a site inspection role. Under the terms of his appointment (Stage K of the old 1982 SFA document), the architect was under duty to visit the site 'as appropriate to inspect generally the progress and quality of work'. Requirements today under the prevailing 'Appointment of an Architect' (SFA/92) are even more onerous: 'Generally inspect materials delivered to site . . . visit the sites of . . . fabrication and assembly of components to inspect . . . workmanship . . . at intervals appropriate to the stage of construction . . . inspect progress and quality . . . to determine . . . generally . . . accordance with the Contract Documents'.

Under the 1982 appointment the architect's defence would in part have turned upon whether he was entitled to rely on the engineer's duty of inspection, or whether his failure as architect to identify independently the sub-contractor's unauthorised departure from the intended structural fixing arrangement was contributory negligence.

The subsequent case upon which I promised to report again involved the apportionment of responsibilities between architect and consultant engineer but differed in that in this instance the engineer had failed to recommend movement joints to the superstructure brickwork when designing foundations where some movement subsequently occurred.

Having found that the engineer had failed to ensure the safety of the structure by designing foundations which allowed excessive movement, the judge went on to consider whether the architect was also negligent. I quote from the judgement: ' (the architect) . . . had an overall general responsibility for the structure and construction details. That was subject to the RIBA Architect's appointment (1982 Edition) by which "the client will hold each consultant and not the architect, responsible for the competence, general inspection, and performance of the work entrusted to that consultant". I have found that (the engineer) contracted with the laintiffs . . . for the provision of calculations and details to enable the architects to proceed with an application for Building Regulations approval . . . the Plaintiffs, having employed the engineers specifically for that purpose through the architects, are contractually bound to look to the engineers and not . . . the architects, who . . . were in turn entitled to rely upon the fact that responsibility had been passed to specialist consultants whom they had previously asked for . . . they referred the question of foundations to those with greater expertise than themselves . . . they questioned the design and received . . . reassurance . . . I find no duty upon these architects to overrule those who . . . have assured that the foundations were adequate'.

This recent judgement is very important for all architects who are unfairly co-joined in claims for damages arising from the error of other consultants. Its early and effective use as a defence argument may save expensive time and fees in unnecessary litigation costs.

Arbitration as an option

In the middle ages, justice could only be obtained outside the feudal system by going before a judge. But it wasn't easy. Judges were peripatetic: that is they slowly advanced around their circuits bringing 'justice' only to the particular parts of the land that they visited. The delay between court visits could be great, and trial costs were enormous.

This kind of justice was totally unsuited to trade, most of which was conducted at fairs and markets. King Edward IV therefore granted a number of charters for private or 'vagabond' courts, the most famous being the Court of Pie Powder (from the French pieds poudreux – dusty feet) which was regularly held at a fair near Winchester. Vagabond courts offered swift decisions; but the chance of a correct decision, or even a fair one, was diminished.

Arbitrations grew out of these rough-and-ready tribunals. The 'judge' was a private person and an expert in the subject matter. He was hired for the task and paid to keep his mouth shut over his decision: arbitration was a commercial business that allowed disputes to be sorted out once and for all – quickly, cheaply, and in private. Was the decision as accurate as a judge's? Possibly not, but high justice was no match for speed and simplicity; and that was what counted.

Arbitrations have a long pedigree, but as with everything involving risk, the tendency has been gradually to make them safer. This has involved the introduction of less rugged procedures, the effect of which had been to lessen the very attributes that made them attractive in the first place. Arbitration and court practices have, in consequence, converged, so that until recently the complaints have been that arbitrations take as long as the courts, that they are as expensive if not more so, and that privacy is a sham.

This downhill slide was only stopped by the publication of the 1996 Arbitration Act, widely acclaimed for putting arbitrations back where they belong: four-square into the domain of trade and commerce. Under the new provisions, properly conducted arbitrations with capped costs should now be subject to disciplined case management and economy.

Cases costing umpteen times as much as the amounts in dispute should become a thing of the past and arbitration will, therefore, once again be able to claim its traditional advantages over litigation.

Meanwhile, in keeping with the changes in the law, through his arbitration advisory committee at the RIBA, institute president David Rock has been pruning his list of arbitrators to a core of the best, and rejuvenating the service by the introduction of strong new blood.

But a word of warning in this age of cost-cutting and streamlining: the RIBA should resist any temptation to 'out-source' this service. Let's not forget: when trouble comes it's much better to have it sorted out by an individual that both parties trust fully rather than by an arbitrator lacking in appropriate expertise. The RIBA has an important role to maintain in this field and you should take the opportunity, when you prepare a building contract or make out a form of appointment, to make sure that it is the president or a vice-president of RIBA who is nominated to appoint the arbitrator. Think about it – a lot could ride on that decision.

Mediation – rough justice, but good!

They say that mediation is no good, but I beg to differ. Earlier this year, a colleague spent a week in closed session with three other parties in a multi-million pound dispute. The mediator was appointed by CEDR, undisputed leader in this sunrise 'profession'.

My colleague likes to think that he can take some credit for the result. But if so, it has much to do with what he said about a discipline in which he, as an architect, has some experience but no qualification: quantity surveying. For the dispute was settled within just a few thousand pounds of what he had argued for.

Did the result have anything to do with the respective liabilities of the parties? Not a lot. Did it have anything to do with the charisma and leadership qualities of the mediator? No. Did it have anything to do with the terror with which each party faced the cost of litigation? In my view, everything.

So here then is a niche. Call it mediation where the mediator, develops inter-party relationships and urges compromise, or the more aggressive Henry Kissinger-style conciliation where the conciliator pays less attention to facilitating direct negotiation but shuttles backwards and forwards between the parties, extracting (and expecting) common sense and compromise as he goes. As long as the costs of litigation remain astronomical, mediation and conciliation will have their place.

Let's not get too excited. Most disputes amount only to a few thousand pounds, and at least one of the parties will be driven as much by wounded pride as by commercial good sense. In such circumstances, mediation or conciliation will, almost certainly, come too late. Moats will have been filled and portcullises lowered – nothing short of a bloodbath will sort them out.

The secret, as with so many failings in human relations, is to halt the damage before it is done; to arrange for an early-day mediation that takes place without it even being noticed.

Who should arrange this virtual mediation? The architect of course; indeed, we do it all the time. We talk to plumbers, bricklayers, steeplejacks, planning officers, valuers; in short, we talk to everyone. And one of the things that we do incredibly well is to apply our skill, knowledge and experience to enable building operations to run smoothly and efficiently, free of the difficulties that arise through failings in communication.

Of course you won't find this responsibility in the forms of appointment, for how would you define it? But it is surely time to recognise the skills we possess, and to champion them.

Sadly, the sudden arrival of statutory adjudication may lessen any widespread willingness within the construction industry to adopt formal mediation and conciliation services. While the monumental and ever-mounting costs of litigation provide sufficient incentive for these processes to have taken hold (and several insurance companies have been insisting on attempts at mediation as a precursor to litigation), adjudication, like mediation, is relatively inexpensive. So it seems almost inevitable that, given its statutory presence, adjudication will succeed at the expense of mediation. This a pity, for mediation is born of agreement whereas an adjudicator's decision is applied with a heavy stick . . .

In my view, matters of difference should, whenever possible, be settled by agreement rather than by decision. On this point Egan surely got it right!

Counting the true cost of litigation

Calls to two barristers' clerks, three barristers and five solicitors have led to some startling conclusions. My quest was to find out whether it would be worth claiming £35,000 unpaid fees in a court case where your client would, in time-honoured fashion, bring a counterclaim of £65,000 in respect of alleged negligence (this is, of course, an imaginary scenario). When asked 'how much it would cost', no straight answers were forthcoming, but in fairness to the legal profession it is very difficult to pre-estimate costs in litigation. However, I've combined all that I've learned, in the table below which shows the likely bill for pursuing such an action to judgement.

Pre-trial		**£**
Partner in solicitor's firm	3 days @ £1,125	3,375
Junior solicitor	7 days @ £565	3,955
Uplift for special attention at 25%		1,833
Expert witness	4 days @ £600	2,400
Counsel's opinion		750

Trial and ancillaries, eight-day trial		
Partner in solicitor's firm	3 days @ £1,125	3,375
Junior solicitor	10 days @ £565	5,650
Uplift for special attention at 50%		4,512
Senior-junior counsel Briefing fee		5,000
Interlocutories, 4 no		4,000
Refreshers	8 days @ £1,000	8,000
Expert witness	4 days @ 600	2,400
Witnesses expenses		750
Solicitor's out-of pocket expenses		1,500
Court fees		400

Total		**£47,900**

Let us now suppose that the 'other side' (your client) accrues similar costs to your own. So the cost of the whole trial, when over, stands at £95,800 – and sorry, the bad news is that you lose: the judge finds that you did not properly complete RIBA Workstage F, and you are not therefore entitled to any fee for that stage (such payment being due only after it is completed).

More bad news unfolds with respect to the counterclaim: it is held that you failed to co-ordinate two aspects of the other consultants' drawings, resulting in a builder's delay. Damages for the full £65,000 are awarded against you. Worse still, because legal costs 'follow the event', your losses amount to a staggering £195,800 before taxation. (Thank heaven for PI!)

What if you win? Let us say that you are entirely successful in your claim. Your client must pay your costs – but not all of them: only those costs that are allowed as being properly necessary to the successful conduct of the case, typically 65 per cent of the total. Thus 'allowed costs' would be £31,135, leaving you to pay the balance of your costs at £16,765.

Considering that your own time involved in briefing lawyers, attending pre-trial meetings, researching the case, preparing statements, and attending trial for four days comes to a total of 136 hours, is it worth it? Success is achieved at huge cost and unacceptable risk. Would you wager £195,000 to win £18,235 at odds of 11:1?

Lord Justice Woolf, examining litigation costs in his report 'Access to Justice', concluded that average costs allowed on cases of this size were 48 per cent of the amount claimed. Costs of smaller cases more often than not exceed the sums in dispute; so although my case is frightening enough, it is not as frightening as most.

Architects' Journal 29.10.98

PART 6

Simple mistakes to avoid

Check your areas – carefully

Many years ago, a client claimed negligence on my part over advice given on building areas. Asked to provide 2,400 square metres of gross internal space on a speculative office scheme, we achieved more than 2,600, this figure appearing on our drawings, the planning application, and in the QS documentation.

With work well advanced on site, the client required confirmation of areas shown on our information, and I erred by reporting some 100 square metres over the amount under construction. Agents for the purchaser subsequently checked areas on site and bingo, we were in dispute.

We contended that the building paid for, against which commercial viability had been checked, had been delivered. The client claimed that discounted terms granted to a purchaser against our latest figures had cost him over £70,000 plus costs – I learned a bitter lesson!

Recently, I acted as expert witness in a dispute between a developer and his architect involving an office scheme in the North-west. The architect, working speculatively, had based his design on an enlarged ordnance map. Area discrepancies were discovered when suppliers of 2,140 square metres of carpet reported that there was only 1,490 square metres of floor! Unfortunately, the architect's drawings, planning application, and the QS documentation all stipulated the larger area: in other words the project's financial viability had never existed.

I identified five separate components of error. First, the architect had misinterpreted the site boundaries. This was compounded by errors made when enlarging the ordnance survey map. Then, after site acquisition and following demolition of existing buildings, a measured survey had been commissioned but on receipt it had apparently been 'put in the bottom drawer' and the architect had continued to use his own incorrect survey.

Later, a series of minor changes each eroded lettable area during design development: toilets and circulation space were added and walls were thickened, especially in the basement where a massive retaining structure was incorporated during design development.

The authorities, of course, also did their worst: an extra (internal) fire staircase had simultaneously increased cost and reduced lettable area, while planners insisted on a section 52 benefit which comprised a public footpath along one boundary of the site, reducing the ground floor area of the building. The architect failed to incorporate the resultant losses into revised area schedules, and gave the client no notice of these changes to the scheme's viability.

The consequences for this client were horrendous and heavy damages were awarded against the surveyor and architect, both cited in the ensuing litigation.

What are the lessons? Certainly, that the basis for calculating gross and net internal areas must be clearly defined for each job; measurement principles vary between surveyors and even the RICS has no single definition. Areas must be calculated, not scaled off prints, and wherever possible they should be qualified with the note 'to be confirmed by site dimensions following construction', although few will let you get away with that one.

Lettable areas in commercial work are critically important: brief assistants well and check their work. Do not let the client, other consultants, or your own team meddle with the figures given without your consent – to do so can have disastrous results. Always check the implications of design changes and inform the client if areas are affected: he may decide to abort the project or, where this is too late, to mitigate losses through initiatives elsewhere.

And finally, there was one other tragic lesson for this architect and his partners in both practice and life: he had allowed his PI policy to lapse following some 20 years of interrupted cover. Failing to heed a warning that his renewal form had not been received (it lay part completed on his desk) he received notification of his alleged error following the lapse and cover was lost. The partnership was, as a result, ruined.

Don't forget those movement joints!

Falling uncomfortably between 'construction' and 'structure', it's amazing how often the old issue of movement joints is overlooked by even the most experienced of practitioners. Engineers frequently fail to alert fellow architects to such requirements, and younger architects have all too often never even heard of them. Indeed my first experience of movement joints was through the timely advice of the engineer Alan Baxter during my first working drawing programme. I do not recall the subject even being discussed during my time at college.

Of course many argue that it is not appropriate to incorporate such basic technical training into an architectural curriculum, and here we encounter the serious division of opinion regarding the range of knowledge and skill that can reasonably be expected of a professional architect.

But 'movement' has been around a long time. The 1963 edition of 'Mitchell's Advanced Building Construction' (first published in 1893) gives a whole section over to this subject. Entitled 'Movement Control', it deals with three aspects: Settlement, Moisture, and Thermal Movement.

Mitchell comments: 'All buildings move to some extent . . . within limits this movement can be accommodated by the fabric without damage to structure or finishes. When greater movement is anticipated, provision must be made for it to take place freely without damage to the building.'

There have, of course, been enormous changes in methods of construction since Mitchell's first work, and of particular relevance to movement issues have been the use of new types of very hard mortars within brickwork. Old and weaker lime mortars tolerated considerable settlement in brickwork without structural cracking, whereas even slight movement in new construction is quickly evidenced by fractures.

Various movement complications arise when adding extensions to buildings. In a 1974 publication, the Brick Development Association advised: ' . . . when adding an extension to an existing building . . . complete separation of old and new work . . . is usually advisable'.

Indeed, manufacturers such as Ibstock show within their technical literature a variety of different types of movement joint.

In developing a 'movement strategy', close collaboration between engineer and architect is needed; the architect should lead on this because his/her concerns extend beyond movement associated solely with structural issues. Within his construction detailing the architect must anticipate what kinds of movement will take place, where, and to what extent. Only then can he produce a workable strategy within his design details.

It is disturbing that the training of architects seems increasingly to take less account of constructional issues at a time when changes in methods and materials of construction demand an ever greater vigilance. The courts will not readily tolerate limp excuses when the writs fly, and on this point we should remember that case law tends to lag some 10 or 15 years behind events in this country: it takes perhaps three years to develop a design, five years for problems to materialise, and five years to get a decision in court.

Only now are we seeing decisions on many failures arising out of changed construction methods of the late 1970s. Architects should, accordingly, take great care to note any changing advices from experts and manufacturers as they may have to demonstrate due competence and duty of care despite fast-changing circumstances.

Dispensations can be dangerous

I got into a terrible pickle over fire regulations during a project for a new warehouse, back in the early 1980s when the old Building Regulations prevailed.

Initially, I had made a mistake relating to the proximity of the new building to the boundary, but what sank me completely was a strategic error on my part when resolving the problem. Briefly, the back of the building had a couple of personnel escape doors from two warehouse units which made up the 3000m2 development. Anxious to maximise lettable space, I had set the building back as close to the boundary as possible. The building was clad in metal which ran to ground level on 'Z' rails spanning between portal frames. The internal arrangements comprised a 1.8m high blockwork wall above which was the usual plasterboard lining – you know the stuff – a typical institutional specification.

Unfortunately, I was over-zealous and set the building too far back, leaving only 780mm between wall face and boundary in lieu of the minimum 900mm requirement. The consequences of this were severe, since the building inspector insisted in these circumstances that the inside blockwork should be constructed up to eaves level (6m) to provide a one-hour fire wall inside the building. The developer client saw this hitch, of course, as an unmitigated disaster. The second mistake concerned my efforts to avoid compliance with this regulation. Initially I argued over the definition of the wall face – inside or outside of cladding profile etc – all to no avail. Next, (ingenious this) I gained the agreement of the owner of an adjoining furniture warehouse to the sale of a 90 metre strip of land 100mm wide in order to 'move' the boundary and obviate the need for the fire wall. (Too clever: it became a ransom strip and the price was raised exorbitantly.)

Finally, I applied for a waiver but this process was too slow and ultimately threatened a delayed handover, so with great reluctance, I was ultimately forced to instruct the construction of the fire wall.

The moral of this story? Well, the regulations have of course since changed, and new processes of relaxation and dispensation replace the old waiver routine, but the essential principles remain the same. Basic arrangements for means of escape must be established at sketch scheme stage as they are fundamental to the building design. Constraints such as proximity to boundaries must be reconciled with constructional and specification arrangements at the detailed design stage and, in order to satisfy the regulations, working drawings and specification must be carried through with a consistent and clear understanding of the criteria that has been applied.

It simply isn't worth relying on waivers, now replaced by 'relaxations' or 'dispensations', on critical issues such as fire regulations. With recent tragedies like King's Cross and Dusseldorf following hard on earlier disasters like Summerland, it is more than a building inspector's job is worth than to give relaxations on these types of issues.

All pretty obvious really, but it's surprising how often architects get tripped up in the same way and end up hopelessly committed to designs that are dependent on just such an inspector's agreement . . .

Don't rely on past work

My good friends at Williams Davies Meltzer, the solicitors, recently sent me a copy of a judgement which has important implications for architects involved in phased construction.

In 1980 the plaintiff had instructed architects and engineers (under separate appointments) to design and oversee a two-storey extension to an existing property. The client subsequently varied his instructions to provide for a two-phased development: the first single-storey phase was to incorporate foundations suitable to carry a second storey, which would be added later. Following completion of phase one a number of cracks began to appear in the new work; some were small, others larger and a cause for greater concern. The client complained but no claim was pursued.

Some five years later, despite these problems, the same professional team was instructed on the second phase. Following completion the ground-floor cracks worsened and more cracks appeared within the new first floor. The client instructed others to investigate: an unacceptably high level of foundation settlement was diagnosed and litigation followed.

Among the many aspects that the Official Referee had to consider was the rights of the client in contract under S.14A of the Limitation Act 1980, and the Latent Damage Act 1986. Together these provide for a limitation period of six years from the date when the cause of action accrues, or three years from the date of the plaintiff's knowledge of a problem or defect – whichever is the longer.

The plaintiff had failed to make a claim against the professionals under the original engagement. When matters finally went to trial in 1995, leave to incorporate this issue into the claims for failures under the second phase appointment was refused. Accordingly, the case rested heavily on whether, under the latter phase of work, the engineers had a duty to re-check the first-phase design and calculations for the foundations.

The engineers claimed that under the first phase, the firm had prepared calculations and obtained consent under Building Regulations for a design which incorporated foundations intended to support a later second-floor addition. They further claimed that they did not have a duty under the subsequent appointment to prepare new calculations to justify the original foundation design, or indeed to check the earlier work – the firm merely had to establish the load-carrying capacity allowed under the original work and design an additional floor that 'fell' within that capacity.

The Referee found against the engineers saying that they had a responsibility as part of the second-phase Building Regulation application and design development to satisfy themselves that the original foundation design work was, in all its aspects, satisfactory. The judgement stated that 'there is a full duty, de novo, to ensure the safety of the structure. The (engineers'). . . choice to rely on the 80/81 design was an attempt to discharge that duty. They chose to put forward in 1986 the negligent design of 1980/81 - in so doing they were negligent . . . '

This has obvious implications for all of us. Clearly, even when a claim would otherwise be barred under the Limitations and Latent Damage Acts, reliance on previous work within a subsequent phase extends professional liability, at least when it is seen as an attempt to discharge a duty to ensure the safety of the structure. Beware!

Problems in the ground

Looking recently at risk, in relation to cost control on building contracts, I reflected on construction problems that I have not been able to anticipate over the years.

Not surprisingly, most of them have been 'in the ground', where the sharp end of uncertainty seems to lie. Indeed my first ever-private commission as a year-out student generated a mini-nightmare. Barely had the new concrete ground slab set in the terraced house that I was renovating when I learned that an existing drain which ran under the property had been condemned due to suspected loose collars by the district surveyor.

My first big project – a 2000 square metre warehouse – produced a real shock. The groundwork sub-contractor was forming excavations for the new portal frame bases when he discovered underground tanks. The GLC petroleum unit was summoned to site where, to my horror, it shut the northbound section of the North Circular Road as a precaution in case of explosion. Asked what investigation I had done into records of previous buildings on the site I had to confess very little. The tanks – there were nine of them – were eventually found to contain not petrol but 'Brylcreem'. It turned out that an earlier building on the site had been a factory for this once popular hair-product.

In Milharbour in London Docklands, there could have been a very serious accident if, having instructed the removal of a reinforced concrete slab on our site, the engineers hadn't undertaken further investigation of local authority records. They discovered that this slab formed a counterbalance to a section that cantilevered some five metres over the water beyond what had been an earlier dock edge. No-one had discovered the cantilever condition during site inspections because it had been formed with a skirt which projected below the waterline at the 'new' water edge.

Those same investigations revealed the foundation arrangements of the previous wharf buildings. We were consequently able to reposition our building, the ground slab of which was entirely suspended on a grid of piles, thus saving the costs of unnecessary breaking-out work.

At Heron Quays (also in Docklands), where we were the first to propose building beyond the quay edge and out over the water, we ran into serious trouble when the third pile began 'bouncing' as it was driven into the dock bottom. We discovered that some preserved bitumen impregnated railway sleepers were causing obstructions (how they got there no-one knew). Removal proved too expensive, so we inserted two piles, one each side of the required position.

A subsequent headquarters project designed by us (and featured as a building study in AJ 2/3/94) also produced unwelcome surprises. Knowing that the land had previously been railway sidings we had anticipated and allowed for removal of contaminated soil. What we didn't expect was the 600mm of oil that constantly filled the basement excavations. Apparently a car scrap-yard had once been located on a nearby site and vast quantities of engine oil, deposited over many years, had percolated into the ground. Showing no respect for legal boundaries the oil had found its way through gravel layers above a clay bed – and into our client's site. This proved to be very costly to remedy.

What are the lessons from such experiences? Certainly, 'desk-top' studies of previous uses going back as far as possible on both your site, and on adjoining sites, are a must. Where possible, physical site investigations – trial bore holes, pits – are also very valuable (though our trial bores all missed the oil!)

But above all, contingency sums must bear sensible relationship to the assessed level of risk. Where information has been unobtainable, and physical investigation limited, larger contingencies are needed. Obviously, one doesn't want to destroy a project's financial viability, but don't let the QS or client persuade you to proceed with inadequate contingency monies. If they do, make sure you spell out the risks to them in writing because otherwise you can rest assured all cost and programme overruns will be blamed on you. Such cases make for very nasty PI claims.

Fire-stopping and site inspection

As the services content of buildings becomes more extensive and complex, arrangements for containing fire and maintaining the integrity of floors and walls that are penetrated by services becomes ever more difficult.

For example, most new student residences are provided with en-suite bathrooms in order to satisfy today's lucrative conference markets where there is a growing demand for self-contained arrangements rather than shared bathroom facilities.

Indeed, it is this demand for en-suite facilities which traditional Oxbridge colleges, or such fine modern work as Denys Lasdun's accommodation at the University of East Anglia, fail to satisfy. By contrast, I recently attended a conference in Birmingham and was billeted in a new student residential block which, albeit of miserably low ambition in terms of design, had clearly met the client's criteria for such accommodation due to its en-suite facilities.

But, as I lay in bed aware of every bodily function performed in the bathroom above, I wondered whether the service ducts had been properly fire-sealed as they passed through the floors.

Such thoughts were prompted by a recent case where a London college had sued its architect and service engineer when it had been discovered that fire-stopping work had been improperly carried out. The fire strategy, in design terms, met the requirements of Building Regulations, and yes the detailing and specification of this immensely complicated area had been thoroughly and properly worked through. But the builder's efforts had left much to be desired.

Fire dampers and intumescent collars were generally in place, but the fire-stopping materials that were supposed to pack the gaps between pipes and concrete slabs at each floor level were, in many cases, poorly installed. Furthermore, holes through the structure had been crudely formed and were often oversized and, as false ceilings were dismantled for inspection, it became evident that substantial and expensive remedial work would be necessary. This was clearly the builder's prime responsibility: there is no way that an architect's duties extend to inspecting every service entry position. (Indeed, I was told that in that case 100 study bedroom units had generated some 1100 'services' penetrations.)

The contractor responsible for that work was one of the more distinguished national building companies whose marketing material has long laid claim (and still does) to traditional values, care and competence. What was found, of course, was the extensive and shameful evidence of slip-shod and incompetent work by slap-happy main and sub-contracting outfits. Typically high on quality assurance boasts, this builder was (and no doubt still is) predictably low on quality delivery.

This raises another point of interest, especially with respect to the future safety of the occupants of such buildings. However expedient it might appear to the QS to transfer responsibility for detailed design and site inspection to the builder, lives are at risk. In this context, can clients really afford to trust builders to carry out work properly, and diligently?

Well, as so many architects know to their cost, the answer to that is all too often no. Buildings are becoming ever more complicated in terms of their services, and the associated construction work is, in consequence, ever more demanding. In relation to matters of fire, there are essentially three stages where care is needed:

● Fire strategy must be resolved – that is, escape routes, compartmentation and general organisation. This must be clearly communicated to the remainder of the design team.

● The detailed arrangements for meeting that strategy must be identified and incorporated into the contract information, and it must be impressed upon the builder that it is the duty of the site team to understand that strategy.

● The work must be carried out competently and thoroughly. As I have implied above, the evidence shows that with grim regularity builders fail abysmally at that last hurdle. As a result, the reduced involvement of architects in site inspection roles, which is ever more a consequence of modern procurement methods, is leaving clients very exposed.

So exposed, in fact, that many owners simply cannot afford to learn how dangerous their buildings really are. Sadly, in some cases, it will be left for a coroner to tell them.

Trouble with rural boundaries

In 1985 a Mr Instey enlarged his garden by purchasing part of a field from Mrs Burton of Home Farm. The land adjoined another field, owned by Wibberley Building Ltd, which had formerly been part of Saverley Green Farm.

The two farms had been divided by a hedge and ditch – the hedge being on the Home Farm side of the ditch. Following acquisition, Instey 'grubbed up' the hedge and erected a fence on the far side of the ditch. Wibberley, believing that the boundary was denoted by the hedge, took legal action and the court found that the strip of land which Instey had 'taken' had indeed belonged to Wibberley. This judgement was affirmed at the subsequent appeal.

But Instey took the matter to the Lords – and won. The ruling was fascinating. The burden had been on Wibberley to show that it had better title, rather than Instey who was 'in possession'. (Possession is, in itself, 'good' title against anyone who cannot show a prior, and therefore better, right to possession: *Asher* v *Whitlock* 1865.)

The question was therefore whether Wibberley had acquired a title in the strip. The title of Saverley Green Farm could be traced back to the 17th century and had always been in separate ownership from Home Farm.

Wibberley's action had been based on the conveyancing documents for the sale of Home Farm to Mrs Burton back in 1975, which contained a plan showing the boundary between the two farms at the hedge centre. This had persuaded the judges in Wibberley's favour both in the initial action, and in the appeal.

In overruling them and finding for Instey, the Lords gave two reasons. First, it must be assumed, in the absence of other evidence, that an owner's land extends to the edge of a ditch on the far side of a hedge. This is because 'a man making a ditch (cannot) cut into his neighbour's soil, but usually cuts to the extremity of his own land (throws) the soil which he digs out upon his own land, and (often) plants a hedge on top of it' (*Vowles* v *Miller* 1810). Draw it for yourself – I had to!

Lord Hoffman could find no evidence that past owners of the two farms had ever challenged or varied this interpretation, so he concluded that the ditch beyond the hedge had originally been dug upon his own land by one of Mr Instey's predecessors in title, and that the boundary was 'beyond that ditch'. Thus the strip of land that comprised both the hedge and ditch belonged to Mrs Burton, who had sold to Instey.

Furthermore, and with resounding logic, Lord Hoffman pointed out that not only could Wibberley not affirm title by reference to its own deeds, but if the sale of Home Farm to Mrs Burton back in 1975 had intentionally excluded the disputed strip of land (as Wibberley alleged) then it remained in the ownership of her predecessor in title (a Mr Beard) who had, in those circumstances, sold her what was logically only part of his land.

Hoffman could see no reason why Beard would have wished to retain such a strip, saying that it was more probable that there had simply been a mistake in the Beard/Burton conveyance plan which was qualified as being for 'purposes of identification only'. The Lords therefore decided that the 1975 intention had clearly been to transfer all the land that comprised Home Farm to Mrs Burton, and that accordingly that part of it which was sold on to Instey must logically include the strip up to the boundary.

So, next time you determine the extent of a rural site look carefully at the boundary – 'your' site might be five metres or so bigger that you think! You'll be flavour of the month if you find a few more house plots in what the client has assumed is a hedge and ditch in the ownership of his neighbour. And if you have ever built on such land? Keep very quiet.

When building inspectors cut up rough

Sod's law has it that when you leave on Friday for your holiday, any problems lurking on your jobs will come winging their way to light the next Monday. Worse, when your colleagues take off hold your breath, for trouble usually comes immediately after their departure.

And so it happened to me some years back. Having wished a colleague bon voyage, I received next day this urgent message: 'Ring the building inspector'. Knowing that we had long ago received Building Regulations consent for a new golf clubhouse, and believing that ongoing local authority site inspections had been without problem, I was completely unprepared for the bombshell that was coming.

The inspector advised that the external walls of this development had been constructed using a different mortar mix from that specified by us, and upon which Building Regulations approval had been granted. He stated that he had brought this to the attention of my office when work was just above dpc level, that he had been advised that we would produce evidence that would allow his authority to accept the changed specification. The inspector further advised that such evidence had (despite ongoing requests) never been forthcoming, and that he was unwilling to let this matter remain unresolved any longer.

Construction was at that time long finished and final fitting-out was almost complete in anticipation of Prince Andrew's imminent arrival to tee off in the morning golf round that would precede his formal opening of the building.

The inspector stated that he was about to advise the client that the building did not comply with the regulations consent notice and that he would commence enforcement proceedings forthwith. I couldn't believe it!

How had this happened? In a nutshell, the builder had decided to use a different mortar specification – relatively weak cement-sand mix, with plasticiser additive, in lieu of weak mix with lime. The inspector had discovered this change and alerted my colleague. Apparently, we had allowed construction to proceed on the basis of this variation, undertaking meanwhile to negotiate and agree the change with the local authority. We had thus embarked on work for which we had assumed unnecessary risk and against which we ultimately had no client instructions and no basis for reimbursement.

Hindsight is precious but we should have instructed compliance with the specification – which would have involved demolition of a week's worth of bricklaying – or at least told the builder that if he continued it was at his risk and for him to gain any necessary consent.

Any involvement by us in gaining such consent should have been on the basis that ongoing construction was entirely at the builder's risk, and that the builder would pay for our 'services'. Why are even the best architects so willing to engage in everyone else's problems without even securing payment for their work?

The construction comprised a 225mm solid wall of flemish bond and an independent dry lining to the inside face. The relatively weak mortar mix was required to maximise flexibility and thus resistance to the cracking that is common in harder mixes, and which can lead to water penetration through capillary action. Furthermore, we had taken particular care in the detailing of lintels and dpc trays with respect to any damp that did penetrate the brickwork and reach the cavity formed by the lining.

Fortunately, I managed to persuade the inspector that I had sufficient expertise to 'underwrite' the builder's variation and accordingly I issued a letter setting out the basis for our confidence in the arrangements, even without the lime additive. This was backed by the assurance of the plasticiser manufacturer that its additive, which aided 'workability' during construction, would have no adverse long-term effect on the mortar's character in terms of its softness and consequent resistance to cracking.

The outcome: successful opening, happy client (blissfully unaware of the problems) and satisfactory building. And my colleague returned off holiday to find his problem solved.

I've started so I'll . . .

A claim for negligence against a design-and-build contractor resulted in a substantial payment by the PI insurers last week. It provides a sobering lesson for us all. The defendant, a Yorkshire-based company, had been appointed by a housing association for new-build sheltered housing for the elderly. The site, within a village, had previously been the subject of much dispute regarding its redevelopment.

After something of a struggle, the design received planning consent and, following routine Building Regulation procedures, the defendant commenced construction. The approval had been based on drawings produced by the contractor, which included plans showing the new scheme together with the buildings on the adjoining sites: on the one side tea rooms and on the other the village post office.

One local resident took a particular interest in the building work. During an evening walk with her dog she noted that the front facade of the new building was being constructed some 500mm forward of the building line of the adjoining post office. Aware that on the planning application the facade had been shown in line with the post office, the resident (helpfully!) brought the matter to the attention of the planning officer. A letter was duly issued requesting that work should stop, pending resolution of the 'difficulty'.

The defendant responded to the local authority saying that in its view the development had proceeded in accordance with the 'approved' design albeit that the drawing error was admitted. Perhaps naively the company sought to regularise matters by issuing a replacement plan showing the relationship with the adjoining building corrected (ie the new facade 500mm forward of the post office). The firm claimed that the adjoining building had been shown in the planning application for 'indicative purposes only', that it had not formed part of the application, and that anyway the irregular building line was more in keeping with the village vernacular.

The planners nevertheless requested a further planning application with respect to this issue, a request which was complied with. In the meantime, and pending a decision at the next available committee meeting, work on the development was 'voluntarily' suspended. The planners' subsequent report recommended consent, but the planning committee unexpectedly refused permission. A horrible impasse had thus been reached.

To cut a long story short, construction remained at a standstill for some eight months pending legal action which culminated in the council issuing a certificate of lawful development. Work ultimately recommenced but following completion of the development the housing association sued the contractor for the losses arising from the contract overrun.

It alleged negligence on four counts: inadequate survey work; misleading/inaccurate drawings with respect to the planning application; inadequate site 'supervision'; and most seriously, inappropriate advice following the Council's 'request' to stop work. However, the ensuing litigation dealt principally with the events following the issue of the council's 'request' to stop work.

And what should the d&b contractor have done, besides carrying out an accurate survey and issuing reliable drawings? Well, it was alleged that on behalf of his client the contractor should have (a) recommended that building work be continued and (b) notified the council that until and unless a formal stop notice was issued, progress on site would be maintained. Under such circumstances, it was claimed that the council would then have been held responsible for the errant issue of a stop notice.

Although this case relates to a d&b contract, it offers important lessons to architects working under conventional appointments. First, make sure of course that your planning applications contain accurate information, and that the builder proceeds in accordance with the terms of the consent. Second, don't let the planners impede progress once a consent has been granted. If they do so, you must make sure that they can be held responsible for the consequential costs of any delay if they have acted outside their authority.

Watch the QS!

A property development executive who rang me up last week claims that, with increasing regularity, his quantity surveyors are reporting tender returns substantially above their estimates. His organisation maintains, alters, and extends a vast range of education buildings – some 220 in all – and it also frequently build new facilities with construction budgets of between £1 million and £5 million.

This client is understandably deeply irritated by appointment terms which entitle his QS to fees as a pre-agreed percentage of the lowest accepted tender – even when that figure is substantially higher than the QS's pre-tender estimate. He doesn't see why he should pay a QS on this basis for poor estimating. I suggested he should get his estimate from the architect instead!

The client is now considering modifying his future appointment terms so that all consultants' fees will be calculated for work up to tender stage on the basis of the approved budget or lowest tender, whichever is the lowest. Thereafter, only fees earnable for the remainder of the appointment would be paid as a percentage of the agreed final contract sum, with no further adjustment being made for the fees earned up to tender stage.

This will of course cause a hoo-ha, and QSs in particular will go through the roof. But they should take this client's criticisms very seriously – he has much to be upset about because the steady increase in project costs that are so common to pre-construction phases are too often a consequence of shoddy professional work. Such poor estimating not only interrupts and delays progress, it also frequently leads to extensive abortive work, damaging the profitability and reputation of the other consultants.

And architects should be sure that they are not blamed, a tactic common amongst so many QS firms, when they are not the cause of estimating errors. They should carefully scrutinise the QS consultant's work at all stages, and never be afraid to get stuck in and identify the cause of poor estimating when it occurs. It's all too easy, when estimating goes wrong, for the QS to be vague and blame others in terms of the quantity or quality of information that has been provided to them. Such-buck passing infuriates clients.

QS firms should also act more professionally by ensuring adequate time for pre-tender information preparation by the design team instead of encouraging impossibly tight programmes and issuing inadequately prepared tender packages as they so often do. Furthermore, they should come clean when they are responsible for the under-estimation – something most QS firms are loathe to do.

I learned recently of a case where the QS had issued tender information containing work from the services consultant that was already much out-dated. When tenders for this renovation project were returned heavily over budget, the QS slyly advised the client that increased costs had arisen because the project team had modified their design and specification work. That was true, but what he didn't say was that the modifications were necessitated by the results of site investigation work and that he, as QS, had been informed of all the changes well before tender packages were sent out. He also omitted to report that he had failed to adjust his tender forecasts, even though the changes had been incorporated into the tender documents.

In short, the QS had neglected to keep the client appraised of issues requiring budget review, while constantly providing outdated and misleading information to the other consultants.

So make sure the QS does his work properly and, above all, ensure that his estimates are based on up-to-date information, that he makes sensible provisions for design development by each member of the team, and that adequate contingency is provided relative to the stage of project development.

Most QS firms will welcome such concern and involvement – those who reject it are to be watched all the more carefully. And those QS firms who pursue exclusive access to clients should be recognised for what they are – mischievous and dangerous charlatans.

Listen to the foreman

My dad – perhaps sensing my impending architectural career – used to tell me the story of his colleague who said, when told by the builder of an error on his drawing, 'If that's what the drawing says, do it'.

That builder cast the mistake in concrete and to this day, the regular stepping rhythm of 'semis' climbing a hillside in Hereford is rudely interrupted by one pair of houses which, sustained by heavy retaining walls, break the natural topography.

Years later Rob Hutson, tha Chelmsford architect who, with typical confidence, counselled an entire generation of AA graduates (his own actually), gave advice which we have often used: find an error early in the contract and unequivocally instruct by AI: 'Take down (that work) and construct as per the contract documentation'. Heavy stuff and not for the faint-hearted!

These issues go to the very heart of leadership – decency, fairness, ability, authority, and clarity. Builders (at least the real tradesmen as opposed to the office-bound surveyors and managers) much appreciate clarity: a site agent once told me that only condemned work received his company's authority to demolish and rebuild: half-hearted memos suggesting repair or requesting 'proposals' are all seen as invitations to argue. A clear AI condemning work avoids debate and facilitates progress: it also sustains standards, for nothing stimulates the tradesman, or his new master the cost surveyor, more than the disheartening and expensive process of demolition.

But such judgements are not easy – they come with experience. And the on-site and often fierce eyeball-to-eyeball contact draws heavily on character, especially if decent relationships based on mutual respect are to be attained and sustained.

The architect's position is made no easier by the increasing tendency of builders to embroil the client or, more frequently nowadays, the project anager in disputes. Copy letters fly the circuit, hackles rise, positions become entrenched and the ugly scenario of 'claims' loom close to the surface of any debate about quality. The architect is often helpless and hapless, as even the consultant QS sits on the fence, or worse, sneaks away and covertly warns the client of the impending consequences of delays on costs. Time is, after all, money where building is concerned.

How do we ensure that young architects are equipped to deal with these circumstances? First, no authority can emerge on either technical or qualitative aspects of construction or contract administration without the confidence that comes with competence. College courses have undoubtedly swung too far away from contract and technology issues in recent decades. I detect a swing back in of some schools but not enough.

Second, professional responsibility and discipline must be assumed during studentship – as is achieved within medicine. The role of the architect, and his/her responsibilities within and to a team must be clearly understood and subscribed to at the earliest career stage..

Finally, offices must set and sustain appropriate standards of competence and integrity. Case studies prepared by students sitting for Part III all too often reveal laissez-faire attitudes and make-shift procedures within their 'year-out' offices during these difficult times of change. That must change too.

Never lose sight of the market

Apparently Concorde uses more oxygen during take-off than the entire Swiss nation breathes in a year. Now, coinciding with Victoria Beckam's adverse comments on safety following the tragic crash at Paris, the prospect of regularly consuming 32,000 gallons of fuel to fly a mere 18 people to New York – as happened again recently on BA scheduled flight 004 – becomes both a reality and a matter of national shame.

That's some 1,800 gallons per person! (A fully loaded Airbus uses around 41 gallons per head for the same journey.) Requiring 90 tons of fuel against a plane weight of 70 tons, with a payload (including passengers) of only 10 tons, Concorde was a flawed and financially disastrous concept from the start. Indeed, the extraordinary thing is not that one has crashed, but that any ever flew. The project should never have seen the light of day.

By the time the sixteenth and last Concorde left Filton in 1978, the aircraft's total development cost exceeded £2 billion (against the originally estimated £160 million), making it perhaps the costliest commercial blunder in history. The anticipated demand had been for 500 planes with investment returned at 150 to 200 Concordes. In the event, only nine were sold before orders collapsed in 1973, and those went to the 'captive' State airlines of British Airways and Air France, who initially took five and four respectively. A further five, though built, remained unsold and two were conveniently written-off after testing.

Not surprisingly, Concorde has been a loser at every turn. With projected sale prices soaring from £10 million to £23 million between 1968 and 1972, and seating a mere 100 people (weighing around 6.8 tons), each plane sold at over twice the cost of a jumbo jet, whil operational outlay per passenger mile was massive. No wonder the options on 74 planes were quickly cancelled: Concorde was in commercial terms, as attractive as a dead duck. Indeed, at no stage in its 40 year life – development, production, or operation – has the project ever showed any prospect of delivering a net profit.

Brian Trubshaw, its ever-loyal first test pilot, revealed the continuing farce recently when trying to allay fears over safety. Maybe no other aircraft in the world does receive better maintenance, but the 56 hours of servicing needed for every hour in flight (eight times more than a jumbo) is merely another measure of Concorde's failure.

Yet despite being consistently and hopelessly unviable, the project was doomed to realisation from the outset. The joint development contract contained no provision for withdrawal, as the Wilson government discovered when facing the massive damages claim payable to the French if Britain backed out – an indignity that would only have been heightened when the French used the money to go it alone. Such were the conditions that effectively spawned the world's most exotic failure, and so it is that last month's tragic crash provided the French with the perfect excuse to call this whole disastrous episode to a halt. But they daren't stop, even now, while the British stubbornly struggle onwards.

The Americans are, of course, far more disciplined about commercial viability, which is why they scrapped their supersonic passenger programme in 1963 and why they have ever since plugged away building the boring, but highly marketable, sub-sonic planes that have enriched their aircraft industry whilst Concorde all but destroyed ours.

And this is probably why, like it or not, so many British developers choose American architects based in London for their building projects: they are objective, disciplined and effective servers of commerce – as they are trained to be. Commercial practice in Britain has learned extensively from the Americans, but much progress has yet to be made – particularly in the areas of cost and risk control during design development.

British architectural practices and schools should take careful stock of that fact and remember the old rule – never lose sight of market demand. The people behind Concorde did, and look what happened.

Conclusion

Advising anyone starting an office today, I would say bill early, bill regularly, and if clients don't pay, stop work. This is important, because only with adequate cash flow can you properly resource your projects. Inadequate resources lead to late information, poor information and ultimately no information – all of which lead to damage to your reputation and claims against you.

Late billing, particularly after you have finished your work, leaves you very exposed. Would a car dealer let you pay for that new BMW a year after you bought it? Late billing inevitably 'invites' clients to use often trumped-up complaints about builder's work as a basis for withholding your money, so get at least 95 per cent of your fees in before issuing the Practical Completion Certificate. Even if you have made mistakes, in theory you are entitled to be paid – that's what you have professional indemnity cover for. The courts don't necessarily see it that way, as they almost always permit clients to offset fees due against their losses. So don't be shy about money. Business clients in particular respect businesses that are serious about fees!

Another good tip is to keep your work for any single client to 30 per cent (or less) of your overall workload. When we worked on Heron Quays (at £60 million it represented 95 per cent of our workload), our client Tarmac Properties only had to sneeze (eg delay the project by a month) and we caught pneumonia!

Never forget to listen to builders – you are part of a team and you need those guys. Arrogant and aloof architects will inevitably one day fall heavily if the builder isn't around to catch them. I always remember one builder who said to me, on discovering a mistake on my drawing: 'Don't worry Paul, there's no mistake in building that can't be put right – it's just a case of who pays'. Then, he kindly took me to lunch. A bribe? I don't know, but it was a good lunch!

On mistakes, never forget that any possible claim must be advised to your PI insurer – immediately. Don't imagine that because you don't think you are at fault you needn't notify them. And never let your PI cover lapse.

In avoiding mistakes, it's worth remembering that many errors arise because you change something (usually at someone else's request) without checking through the implications. Changes, especially in rushed scenarios, are dangerous. Be careful: if you change that specification, does it affect your Building Regulations consent? If you alter that design do you need to re-negotiate with the Planners? Does that alteration to the paint schedule affect your warranty? Will those changes to area affect the project's financial viability? Also, always remember to feed in new information at the appropriate time; don't stick that site survey drawing in the drawer – use it. And always fight for adequate time to do your work – in particular don't be persuaded by the QS or anyone else to issue abbreviated information where this introduces unacceptable risks.

Always get a proper appointment in writing. (The ARB Code of Conduct requires this anyway.) And be careful, for you need a client's reply that states unequivocal acceptance of your proposal. A letter that says, 'I generally accept your proposed appointment terms but wish to discuss some points' is no good. Discuss them now. Tie them down. And where you are doing speculative work, make sure that you have a satisfactory fee agreement in place that defines the point at which fees become payable, the amounts that will be due, and the basis of your future appointment. You weaken your negotiating position if you leave such details until after you have won that development bid for your client. He is not as generous (or stupid) as you. Clients (especially developers) see life differently.

But most of all, enjoy yourselves. We operate within an extraordinary industry, at a time of enormous change. We are part of a wonderful profession which faces, perhaps, the most difficult challenges of its entire history: that is, the demand for an ecologically sustainable building programme for our towns and cities.

Ours is a profession of big names, star names and inevitably, a mass of lesser-known and unknown personalities. But most of us are bound by two key characteristics: an unyielding optimism combined with the will to see good architecture realised in all its varieties.

Ours is a warm and generous profession. For me, being part of it, and having had the privilege of writing a weekly column for so long, has been one of the greatest pleasures of my life.